PRAISE FOR

WOMA
WALK
THE LINE

"A rhapsodic, moving look at music and its transformative power."
—*People*

"A new collection of personal essays on the transformative impact of women in country music aims to change the narrative."
—*The Washington Post*

"An exploration of that liminal space between the artist's intention and the listener's reception."
—*The Oxford American*

"These are personal essays about influence and inspiration . . . at their best, they shine their light on the story and the storyteller equally."
—*The New York Times Book Review*

"The stylistic line from Maybelle Carter through Dolly Parton on up to Taylor Swift isn't a straight one, and the intention of this absorbing anthology isn't to pretend that it is . . . intimate, inspirational essays."
—*Mojo*

"There's probably no better time for *Woman Walk the Line* . . . the groundbreakers continue to strike many chords."
—*Rolling Stone*

"The deeply personal pieces often feel like the authors are cracking open a secret chest, sharing treasured glimpses into their true selves."
—*Salon*

AMERICAN MUSIC SERIES

Jessica Hopper and Charles L. Hughes, series editors

Stephen Deusner, *Where the Devil Don't Stay: Traveling the South with the Drive-By Truckers*

Eric Harvey, *Who Got the Camera? A History of Rap and Reality*

Kristin Hersh, *Seeing Sideways: A Memoir of Music and Motherhood*

Hannah Ewens, *Fangirls: Scenes from Modern Music Culture*

Sasha Geffen, *Glitter Up the Dark: How Pop Music Broke the Binary*

Hanif Abdurraqib, *Go Ahead in the Rain: Notes to A Tribe Called Quest*

Chris Stamey, *A Spy in the House of Loud: New York Songs and Stories*

Adam Sobsey, *Chrissie Hynde: A Musical Biography*

Lloyd Sachs, *T Bone Burnett: A Life in Pursuit*

Danny Alexander, *Real Love, No Drama: The Music of Mary J. Blige*

Alina Simone, *Madonnaland and Other Detours into Fame and Fandom*

Kristin Hersh, *Don't Suck, Don't Die: Giving Up Vic Chesnutt*

Chris Morris, *Los Lobos: Dream in Blue*

Eddie Huffman, *John Prine: In Spite of Himself*

John T. Davis, *The Flatlanders: Now It's Now Again*

David Cantwell, *Merle Haggard: The Running Kind*

David Menconi, *Ryan Adams: Losering, a Story of Whiskeytown*

Don McLeese, *Dwight Yoakam: A Thousand Miles from Nowhere*

Peter Blackstock and David Menconi, founding editors

WOMAN WALK THE LINE

HOW THE WOMEN IN COUNTRY MUSIC CHANGED OUR LIVES

Edited by

Holly Gleason

UNIVERSITY OF TEXAS PRESS  AUSTIN

Copyright © 2017 by Holly Gleason
All rights reserved
Printed in the United States of America
First edition, 2017
First paperback reprint, 2021

Requests for permission to reproduce material
from this work should be sent to:
    Permissions
    University of Texas Press
    P.O. Box 7819
    Austin, TX 78713-7819
    utpress.utexas.edu/rp-form

♾ The paper used in this book meets the minimum
requirements of ANSI/NISO Z39.48-1992 (R1997)
(Permanence of Paper).

Library of Congress Cataloging-in-Publication Data

Names: Gleason, Holly, editor.
Title: Woman walk the line : how the women in country
    music changed our lives / edited by Holly Gleason.
Other titles: American music series.
Description: Austin : University of Texas Press, 2017. |
    Series: American music series
Identifiers: LCCN 2017009448
    ISBN 978-1-4773-2258-1 (pbk: alk. paper)
    ISBN 978-1-4773-1489-0 (library e-book)
    ISBN 978-1-4773-1490-6 (nonlibrary e-book)
Subjects: LCSH: Women country musicians—
    United States. | Women singers—United States. |
    Country musicians—United States. | Singers—
    United States.
Classification: LCC ML394 .W67 2017 |
    DDC 781.642092/52—dc23
LC record available at https://lccn.loc.gov/2017009448

doi:10.7560/313916

CONTENTS

---

ele

INTRODUCTION

———

Tonight I wanna do some drinkin'
I came to listen to the band
Yes I'm as good as what you're thinkin'
But I don't wanna hold your hand
And I know I'm lookin' lonely
But there's nothin' here I wanna find
It's just the way of a woman
When she goes out to walk the line
                    —EMMYLOU HARRIS, 1985

Maybe it was the tomatoes. Not the homegrown kind
Guy Clark used to sing about, but the comment some
radio programmer made about a woman's place on
country radio—women being the tomatoes, 'cause unless you
have some thick delicious mozzarella, you wouldn't make them
the bulk of your salad.

Perhaps it was my students, the young people in my Music
Criticism class, part of Middle Tennessee State University's
fabulous Recording Industry Management program. Theoreti-
cally passionate about music, they struggle to articulate why
they love the artists they do. Or, as the reigning Band Aid, Sap-
phire—in Cameron Crowe's coming-of-age-as-a-baby-rock-
critic Academy Award–winner *Almost Famous*—says, malign-
ing the next wave of groupies, "These new girls don't know what
it means to be a fan, to love some band or some silly little piece
of music so much it *hurts*."

Or maybe it's just the fact that whenever you want to know
someone, I've found all you have to do is ask them what artist
they love . . . really, *really* love. Even the most passive people can

surprise you with their knowledge of and passion for an unlikely purveyor of song.

Quite possibly, it was all of the above that led me to chase, badger, and exult in what you now hold in your hands. *Woman Walk the Line: How the Women in Country Music Changed Our Lives* represents so many things. Part history, part criticism, these are large chunks of life pulled through the prisms of the twenty-seven artists who are singled out. It matters less when, where, why, or how it happened; the point is that every last one of the women celebrated in these essays stirred the writers, in many ways changing their lives forever.

And women live lives, make no mistake. They fall in love, shatter to pieces, work like dogs, refuse to be bound by conventional wisdom, and lift other people up so they can be more than they ever imagined. They get drunk; they go to church; they have babies; they bury friends. Along the way, they keep striving—and even when spinning out, they try to always maintain the essence of who they are.

And so it is a diverse group of artists, activists, and writers who tackled the task of explaining that one country female who connected with them. For these contributors, it was the presence, the moxie, the music that brought their own quests to life.

For a Long Island girl in satin disco pants, Dolly Parton showed that you could write your own songs *and* wear high heels while scaling the ladder of success, whether you were a superstar or a high-level TV news producer. A Texas girl inhabiting a *Friday Night Lights* world found solace and grounding on an eighth-grade trip to New York, during the heyday of grunge and Guns N'Roses, through the mother/daughter duo the Judds— and still hears *home* in their records today.

Tanya Tucker, Linda Ronstadt, and k.d. lang exuded sexuality for a wallflower, a bohemian, and a soon-to-be-out queer, while Terri Clark embodied the southern girl's challenge of staring down the double standard without losing her spunk, and Patty Loveless's pluck led an award-winning journalist from the *Miami Herald* to pursue a whole other life in Nashville,

Tennessee. Whether it's the then-seventeen-year-old Taylor Swift writing about another precocious superstar named Brenda Lee, or Rosanne Cash eulogizing her stepmother, June Carter Cash, in front of a capacity church, there is recognition—woman to woman, generation to generation—and inspiration to be found here, not just in these women's artistry but in their humanity.

Starting with Maybelle Carter—first heard next to a campfire and recognized by a soon-to-be MTV exec as the root of practically all music—this book moves through some of the genre's superstars, but also its lesser-known heroines. Neither a definitive history nor the final word on which artists matter most, it offers a core sample of women who made country music, seen through the eyes of some of their greatest appreciators. Regardless of her multiplatinum sales status or her relative obscurity, each artist here matters deeply to the woman writing about her. That immersion allows each writer to move beyond the facts to the personal sense of what the music means, arriving at a place where music's deeper impact can be felt in one particular life.

For one writer looking to realign her place in the world, Rosanne Cash served as a paragon of metamorphosis and a beacon of honoring who you truly are. Loretta Lynn embodied a social revolution already past—and then became real to a young critic in her own time. For many of the writers, the entry point *was* youth—that time when the world is new, when sifting the various aspects of who they are going to become seems overwhelming; for them, the music served as a trail of crumbs or a catalyst to their future.

But for some writers, the revelation came later: the women they celebrate opened veins of grief. Patty Griffin, an Americana icon and a much-covered songwriter, offered a balm for post-9/11 trauma and set the writer's mind—and sense of ambition—at ease, while Emmylou Harris gave an activist access to her emotions when she was struck numb because of sudden, extreme mourning.

For other writers, their country heroines broke the ground

that everyone else trod after. Lil Hardin, a largely unknown creative force, was a pilot light for a black woman drawn to the ostensibly white world of country music that should have been closed to her; with Hardin as her inspiration, this overachiever went from Harvard to songwriting, from the *New York Times* Best Seller List to a development deal with Quincy Jones and documentary work for Ken Burns.

As interesting as the female songwriters, singers, and musicians are, the contributors are as fascinating in their own right. They have won Grammys, Pulitzer Prizes, Emmys, James Beard Awards, ASCAP Foundation Deems Taylor Awards for literary excellence, BMI Millionaire Awards for songwriting, fellowships, and grants. They have exceeded expectations in many ways, and certainly conventions. And when you talk to *any* of them, there is always "that" artist—the one whose music they can go on and on about, the one who transfixed them with what her persona or voice represented, how she looked or the way she lived.

"That" artist, the one who stopped them in their tracks, who slowly got under their skin. No matter how it happened, the listener was never the same after being exposed. It's magic, the way the music marked these women and the way the artists became their doppelgängers, guiding lights, and inspirations.

Country music, defined as simple songs about real life, is in many ways women's music. From the moment Kitty Wells sold a million copies of "It Wasn't God Who Made Honky Tonk Angels," the female voice has been known for deep truth-telling. Between Loretta Lynn's "Fist City" and "Don't Come Home A-Drinkin' (With Lovin' on Your Mind)" and Tammy Wynette's "Stand by Your Man" and "'Til I Can Make It on My Own," the polemics of the male/female relationship in the sexual revolution were covered. Smart, cool, brash, tough, mysterious, sassy, sexual, earthy, young, maternal, it's all here—in a way you won't find in any other genre.

At a time when Google search and Wikipedia fill in for flesh-and-blood experience, and when Spotify and Pandora supply only an algorithmic sense of what music is, there is still nothing like personal witness when it comes to understanding why an artist matters. It's not the song construction or the facts of the life lived that get to where the music starts, either, but more the way the music stains people's lives and changes their trajectories: that's what makes these artists indelible.

When the sound, a voice, reaches directly to your core, your gut, your heart, your dreams—especially the dreams you didn't even know you had—that's when music matters. Strength, courage, healing, vitriol—any of these can emerge for listeners when they don't even know that's what they need.

A male friend who used to be a punk god once told me he loved hanging with "the girls" back in the day, because he felt like he got an understanding of the female psyche. Not quite a trip behind enemy lines, but more a glimpse behind the curtain all women are taught to draw across their true emotional selves, to keep from being labeled with all the marginalizing words people love to hurl: *messy, inconvenient, castrating, hysterical, weak, meek*—and yes, *nasty*.

As in the Emmylou Harris song cited above, from her purportedly autobiographical song cycle *The Ballad of Sally Rose*, women's emotions don't undermine their ability to get it done. Indeed, if they step back and breathe it in, it may well be the reason they can and they do accomplish so much. As much as the artists themselves, that's what this collection celebrates.

Holly Gleason
January 2017
Somewhere on the road

...le Carter | Lil Hardin | Wanda Jackson | Hazel

...Cash | Brenda Lee | Bobbie Gentry | Loretta Ly...

...n | Emmylou Harris | Barbara Mandrell | Tanya

... | Linda Ronstadt | Rosanne Cash | The Judds | k...

...ms | Mary Chapin Carpenter | Patty Loveless | Sha...

...n Krauss | Terri Clark | Taylor Swift | Kacey Musg...

...annon Giddens | Patty Griffin | Maybelle Carter | J...

...a Jackson | Hazel Dickens | June Carter Cash | Bre...

...Gentry | Loretta Lynn | Dolly Parton | Emmylou H...

...a Mandrell | Tanya Tucker | Rita Coolidge | Linda

...anne Cash | The Judds | k.d. lang | Lucinda William...

...in Carpenter | Patty Loveless | Shania Twain | Alis...

...lark | Taylor Swift | Kacey Musgraves | Rhiannon Gi...

...y Griffin | Maybelle Carter | Lil Hardin | Wanda

MAYBELLE CARTER

The Root of It all

CARYN ROSE

I found American folk music through what seemed like an unlikely back door: discovering Woody Guthrie via Pete Seeger via Bob Dylan while I was at Girl Scout camp. So much of what you sang at camp in the seventies had to do with whether or not your counselors played guitar. If they didn't, you would still get access to the unexpected—that's where I learned "Froggy Went A-Courtin'"—but a guitar gave you more options. Because of cool, guitar-toting counselors, over the course of a series of summers I learned all of the verses to "This Land Is Your Land" alongside "Sloop John B," "Beautiful People" next to "Joe Hill," "Heart of Gold" after "I Shall Not Be Moved," and "The Bear Went over the Mountain" with "Keep on the Sunny Side." To me they were all just camp songs, until I turned on the radio and there were Neil Young and the Beach Boys singing the songs I had learned around a campfire, or hiking the Appalachian Trail, or walking to and from the dining hall three times a day. (A singing camper was a happy camper.)

As a preteen, I was voracious about music, consuming anything I could get my hands on, sleeping with the radio under my pillow, listening to AM and FM and WCBS Golden Oldies and world music shows on public radio. I read at a level far above my grade (thanks to my mother), so my parents would buy me any music history books that looked substantial, and I would go to the library on weekends to peruse the stacks or, after I learned how to use the *Readers' Guide to Periodical Literature*, thread microfilm into one of those old pyramid projection machines. But it wasn't until I heard Joan Baez singing "Joe Hill" on the Woodstock soundtrack that I realized that there was something going on with some of those songs. I started looking around. Bob to Pete to Woody. *I knew those songs.*

I began tracing the threads of every song I knew to try to find their origins. In the process, I was learning about the history of American recorded music, the history of rock & roll, the history of folk. One Saturday, as I was flipping through a book, I came upon a black-and-white photograph of a woman holding a guitar with absolute comfort, looking impassive—this was not a big deal to her—and very much at home. The caption told me that she was named Maybelle Carter, and I wanted to know more about her. I wanted to know more not because I wanted to play guitar, but because I loved music and wanted to feel like there was a place somewhere in there for me, even as just a music fan.

Every time I talked knowledgeably about music—and I held forth extensively in order to prove I actually knew what I was talking about—I was viewed as a unicorn, and had to listen to yet another proclamation of "You sure know a lot about music, for a girl." So I was looking for all the women I could find. Role models, sisters, compatriots. Punk rock would come a year or two later, and I didn't see myself in Janis Joplin or Grace Slick. Heart was basically Led Zeppelin, whom I didn't like at all (shhh, don't tell anyone). I hadn't found Joni Mitchell yet. There were not a lot of options.

Maybelle Carter wasn't hesitant or asking permission to be there, she was there; she wasn't backing up some dude, she was the musician. I had librarians who loved me and did interlibrary loans for record albums—those early seventies RCA compilations of the Carter Family—so that I, headphones on, could hear her play, sitting in the library on a rainy Saturday, wishing for clues in the album covers that would tell me more about her. The librarians helped me find paragraphs or sections of books about her, covering it up with "This is research for a school paper" when quizzed. All I could tell them was, "I just want to know more about this woman and who she was and why she did what she did." We were in cahoots; it wouldn't be the last time that I learned that other women will help you if you need to find something out, but it was one of the first conscious moments of solidarity for me. I couldn't explain why I needed to know more, just that I did. I wasn't asking permission, and they weren't requiring me to. I needed to know; that was enough. They legitimized my quest.

I stumbled onto the Carter Family around the same time that I began to connect the dots about Stax and the blues, when I was digging down to find the roots of everything, to try to understand where what I listened to came from, to identify a song heard in passing on the radio—you would try to be near a phone to call the disc jockey, or walk into a record store and describe it as best you could. I didn't see it as country music, I just saw it as early music, roots music before that was any kind of a thing: the origins, the basics.

My parents were from Brooklyn and Chicago; my father loves news talk radio, but my mother hung out in jazz clubs listening to Ahmad Jamal, and she loved Frank Sinatra and Johnny Mathis. I grew up on show tunes. What we didn't listen to was country music, in any way, shape, or form. It wasn't just that my mother didn't like it, it was about class: having stepped up out of the working class to the middle class, there were things you did not do. You didn't watch *Hee Haw*, and you didn't listen to country music. But I wanted to listen to everything, just because I could. I was afraid I would miss something, which is why I walked around with the radio glued to my ear or under my pillow or listened via a surreptitious earbud while riding in the family car.

I would come back to Mother Maybelle over the years, as she began to get the credit and recognition she deserved. I loved the story about her taking over the family business after A. P. Carter and her sister (then A. P.'s wife) Sara left, starting the Carter Sisters with her daughters—Anita, Helen, and June—because this was a way to earn money for the family and there was money to be made. She took control of the Carter Family legacy as sure as any PR expert. When June met Johnny Cash and later married him, the Carter Sisters became part of that path as well. When there was a folk revival in the sixties and renewed interest in the songs the Carter Family played, Maybelle managed to find a way to be a part of that, too. She managed to hustle without drawing attention to the fact that that was, in fact, what she was doing, because ambitious women were not well thought of. She never said such a thing, but it is part of the unwritten code all women know and have handed down through generations.

Maybelle Carter didn't just play guitar, she played guitar when it wasn't considered a serious instrument, when it was considered a backing instrument at best. Maybelle Carter not only played guitar, she invented and established a playing style—now known as the "Carter scratch"—that became a fundamental of country music. She would strum the rhythm and pick out the melody with her thumb in a rolling, fluid motion that might look simple, but there are many established country musicians in this day and age ready to tell you in no uncertain terms that it is not. She was a *lead guitarist*. She wasn't decorative. She wasn't optional. She was the main musician, and she acted like it. She didn't stomp around insisting on credit, she just showed up and played.

I loved the stories of her smoking and driving the van, being a real road warrior, and I tried to imagine the freedom that playing music gave her, a freedom that most women in that day and age could not even imagine. Maybelle Carter was self-taught, she was playing banjo when she was three years old, she was voracious, she kept the music and songs and the tradition going. She just got up every day and worked. And there is no way it wasn't hard, and there's no way she didn't go through what every woman at the forefront of anything goes through, but she just kept doing it anyway, like so many women before her and after her.

In an interview with *Billboard* in 1968, she told a story about having to ride on the running board of the Model-T they used for touring, because the lights were out and it was the only way they would get home. She tells it matter-of-factly—yes, it was hard; yes, I had to do these things, but it's just a thing that they had to do to be on tour, to take their music to the audiences where they were. (She also mentions in that interview how, if they got two hundred people at a show, she considered it a success, because most of those people had to walk to get there.) The phenomenal amount of just plain life she had to get through just to be able to do her job is more than most of us face in a lifetime. It's a good thing to remember when you think things are getting hard.

LIL HARDIN

———

That's How I Got to Memphis

ALICE RANDALL

I'm just another brown girl all full of vim, chocolate gal, good intentions.

—LIL HARDIN

L il Hardin is an invisible woman, an invisible black gal, at the beginning of the history of recorded country music, changing everything that came after: Lil Hardin is the piano player on Jimmie Rodgers's "Blue Yodel #9."

I don't remember not knowing Lil Hardin. The year I was born, 1959, in Motown, a songwriter's town, Ray Charles covered "Just for a Thrill" (a song Hardin wrote and recorded first, in 1936) on his album *The Genius of Ray Charles*.

Around my way, the black Detroit neighborhood just off the John C. Lodge Freeway, Lil Hardin and her hit song "Just for a Thrill" got talked about, that year and for years to come. *The Genius of Ray Charles*, released in October of 1959, six months after my birth, was a foundation text. Everything about it was worthy of discussion and examination.

There were two women on the album. Both wives. Lil Hardin Armstrong and Fleecie Moore. Lil was Louis Armstrong's second wife; Fleecie Moore was Louis Jordan's third wife. My daddy liked to say his two sisters were as different as sugar and shit. He said the same about Lil and Fleecie. Lil was the sugar.

My daddy talked like that: sugar and shit. To understand me, you have to understand the place and the language of the place I come from; you have to understand what it meant to be George Randall's daughter, and Bettie Randall's daughter; you have to understand what it means to have a Lil Hardin song save you.

I was the Motown black girl who took a Beatles lunch box to her all-black Lutheran private-school kindergarten in Detroit, but I was also the daughter of Alabama-born dry cleaner George Randall, who believed Louis Jordan had much to do with the invention of rock & roll; who had once wooed Anna Gordy, Barry's sister; who claimed that Marvin Gaye had pressed clothes for him to make extra money; and who began certain reminiscences by saying, "When I was a shoeshine boy, and Anna was a whore"— meaning, back in a past that must necessarily be forgotten, because you did whatever it was that needed doing, back in that time, to get to this better time.

In that place, and time, and language, Lil Hardin Armstrong was the country sugar.

In my father's telling, everybody knew that Fleecie never wrote a syllable or a note, a lyric or a bar of music, or any other part of a song in her life. Louis Jordan just put her name on huge songs, including "Let the Good Times Roll," to get out of some publishing company trouble, contract trouble; and—according to my father—"the bitch jumped up and stabbed him!"

On the other hand, Daddy declared that Lil Hardin Armstrong wrote every lick of "Just for a Thrill," and some "peckawood put his name up there with hers." To prove his point, my father dug out a copy of an earlier recording of "Just for a Thrill" that my aunt Mary Frances owned. That 1937 Decca recording of "the very same song" had only Lil's name on it.

I learned to read by reading song labels and by having my Daddy read to me from the "colored paper," the *Michigan Chronicle.*

Daddy prepared me, like he knew it was coming, for the theft and racism I might encounter in the music business—by telling me from the jump about the theft and racism Lil Hardin endured, and eclipsed, in the music business. And far more significantly, Lil Hardin's lyric "I was merely a toy, a plaything . . .

just for a thrill you made my life one sad song" prepared me to transcend sadism and resist objectification.

My aunt Mary Frances's stereo and her large collection of vinyl records were the heart of her house—my first home. I don't remember Mary Frances ever turning on her giant television. We didn't gather round the television or even the dining table. We gathered round the stereo, singing "Just for a Thrill," singing "God Bless the Child," singing "sometimes I feel like a motherless child, a long, long way from home."

I couldn't understand that song. I had a crazy mother. I thought being a motherless child a long way from home would be a good thing, a safe thing. And I knew, as soon as I got old enough to learn what the word "thrill" meant, that Lil Hardin was telling the big truth about Mama and me when she wrote, "just for a thrill you made my life one sad song."

That was powerful. Having my trauma narrated, the pain of recognizing that some people treat others like toys because it gives them pleasure, eased my trauma. Lil did not erase my trauma, but she sure as sugar eased it. Lil's lyrics, and Lil, had power. Not the power to change what happened, but the power to change surviving to thriving simply by making the cry beautiful, making the cry smart, making the cry about more than what caused you to cry, making the cry the place you found yourself, and acknowledging what you deserved—and what you lacked.

I wanted to be a songwriter from early days. I wanted to speak for those who could not speak for themselves—not as a lawyer, as my daddy instructed me while I was still in a crib, and not as a novelist, for I did not know in my early days what novels were. But I knew what songs were, and I had discovered from the sounds of Lil Hardin that songs and songwriting were a kind of alchemy before I knew the word *alchemy*.

Lil Hardin played piano. Hardin read music. Hardin wrote hit songs. Hardin sang. Hardin was a bandleader. And Lil Hardin Armstrong was the most significant manager Louis Armstrong ever had, the one who changed the way he dressed, his position in the band, his understanding of his place in the horn pantheon.

These were the accomplishments that got her into the Memphis Music Hall of Fame. These were the accomplishments that have awed me and others over the decades. These were the reasons why the great blueswoman Alberta Hunter loved to perform on a stage with Lil. People remember Lil Hardin, sometimes for what she herself contributed to jazz and to blues, and sometimes for what she contributed to her second husband, Louis Armstrong. But people forget her contributions to country music. Or maybe it's worse than forgetting—maybe they just don't know about them in the first place.

I don't forget. Lil Hardin changed my life. Many times. I took piano lessons and was no good. And I still can't sing. But I could write, and my first lemonade stand was pretty successful, so I figured I'd follow her into songwriting and business. See it, be it. I followed Lil Hardin into the heart of the country canon.

Let me say it again, since it warrants repeating: Lil Hardin is the piano player on Jimmie Rodgers's "Blue Yodel #9."

What this means to me is that we, black women, have been present in country since almost the very beginning, at least since 1931. It's a small circle. Linda Martell singing on the stage of the Opry in 1969 and recording for Plantation Records: I wrote about her for the *Oxford American*. She meant something to me. The Pointer Sisters had a hit, "Fairytale," on country radio in 1974, when I was in high school. Two of them wrote the song, and the whole group recorded it at Quadrophonic Studio, just a few blocks from where I now live in Nashville. Tina Turner recorded a country album on United Artists Records later that same year. She covered Hank Snow's "I'm Moving On," Kristofferson's "Help Me Make It Through the Night," and Dylan's "Tonight I'll Be Staying Here with You" on her way to earning her country bona fides. Micky Guyton visited my Vanderbilt class on the black presence in country music in the winter of 2015, and I noticed one of my students, a brilliant black woman, on her phone. Finally she twirled the phone to me to reveal that she was Facetiming with her sister, a huge Mickey Guyton fan. Mickey means more than many realize to brown girls across the nation. And I've been loving on Rhiannon Giddens for a good long time, even before "Genuine Negro Jig," an elemental country classic, came out. Finally, Beyoncé closing down the 2016 CMA Awards singing "Daddy Lessons" was a sight to see.

All these amazing black women doing country their way, braiding evangelical Christianity and all kinds of black musical aesthetics, mean a lot to me—but none of them means quite as much as Lil Hardin. People often think of me as a trailblazer. Lil was the trailblazer.

Everything about the woman inspires me. Much about her life resonates with my own: her unorthodox approach to the keyboard; her hyperbolic identity, equal parts street (in her case, Memphis's Beale Street; in my case, Detroit's Black Bottom Chene Street) and academy (in her case, Fisk; in my case, Harvard); her ambitious mother (in her case, endearing; in my case, evil); her early black arts training (in her case, at Memphis's Hooks School of Music; in my case, at the Detroit Ziggy Johnson School of the Theater).

Now, Lil wasn't my only influence. During my college days I got interested in American metaphysical poetry. About the same time, I first tried my hand at screenwriting—before the advent of word processing programs. To distract myself from the trials of screenplay formatting, I started listening to a country station. It struck me strong that songs like "Drop Kick Me Jesus Through the Goal Posts of Life" were really a form of metaphysical poetry. And I knew the banjo was an African instrument. I also knew bluegrass had more than a little something to do with jazz. Country always seemed to me to be blacker than realized, more feminist than realized, more significant than acknowledged.

I arrived in Nashville in March of 1983.

I drove down the night after attending the twenty-fifth-anniversary CMA concert at DAR Constitution Hall. My freshman year roommate's mother was the managing director of ASCAP and had introduced me to a few Nashville folks. One of them, Buddy Killen, then president of Tree International Publishing, gave me the tickets. President Reagan and Vice

President Bush were in attendance. I sat almost exactly opposite Reagan. I was wearing a size-six black silk Vicky Tiel dress purchased in London for the occasion. The dress had western fringe. Looking back, I suspect I looked like an expensive barmaid. When the show was almost over, Reagan took to the stage.

"And I also would like to congratulate the Country Music Association on its twenty-fifth anniversary. For a quarter of a century, CMA has been encouraging, developing, and promoting the musical sound that comes straight from America's heart . . . But the best thing about country music is its people—"

Lil Hardin was one of those people. Raised in Memphis by a grandmother who had been a slave in Mississippi, Lil Hardin effectively constructed a life of creative liberation, inspiring others to follow after her—not in her footsteps, but in her spirit.

The Friday morning after the big concert, I headed out, driving to Nashville. One of the six people I knew in the city to say hello to suggested I go see a little rockabilly band led by an amazing thirty-something songwriter that was playing a hot new club on the south side of town. I intended to see Steve Earle at the Blue Bird Café that night but never found the place, because I wasn't looking in a strip mall. I found him Saturday night.

A few weeks later I wrangled Steve's phone number out of one of the people I knew in Nashville and called him up. When I expressed an interest in writing with him, he demanded to know how I got his number and started ranting at me. He was having a bad day. Strange women were calling and his car was broke down. I asked him if he needed a ride. He said yes.

The rest is a foundation block of my country music history. I picked Steve up from an apartment on Belmont Boulevard and dropped him at LSI Studio. When he got out of the car I handed him a cassette with a song on it that I had cowritten with a woman named Diana Haig. I believe the song was called "Dangerous Curves." Whatever kind of bitch he hadn't called me when I originally asked him about cowriting he called me then, and underlined it by slamming the car door. A week later he called me. He said I was going to be a country songwriter one day and he was going to help me. Later I asked him why he did it. You were black and from Harvard, he said; it was a novelty. Soon I was rich enough in demos and cowriters that a different legendary Texas songwriter snarled, after meeting me, something like, "I can't believe I've lived long enough to have to compete for cuts with colored girls from Harvard." Except I don't think he said colored and I know he didn't say black.

I didn't bat an eyelash. I thought of all that Lil Hardin had endured on the Chitlin Circuit. Then, like Lil, I had a stroke of good fortune, and it came from California.

I met Californian Mark Sanders at a Music Row weinie roast and went on to write with him more than I wrote with any other writer. He would write his biggest hit, "I Hope You Dance," with my daughter's Saturday night babysitter, Tia Silliers, after I introduced them. But long before that, Mark would write his first B side of a number-one single with me, "Reckless Night," and his first top-ten hit with me, "Girls Ride Horses Too."

I was the founder of the publishing company MidSummer Music, which collaborated with Major Bob Music to publish Garth Brooks at the beginning of his career, as well as Mark Sanders. Some of Garth's most famous songs are in the Mid-Summer catalog: "Unanswered Prayers," "The River," "What She's Doing Now," and "Like We Never Had a Broken Heart." Mark sang at my first wedding. Mark and Garth are now in the Nashville Songwriters Hall of Fame.

When Odie Lindsey introduced me as a member of a panel on Americana music in 2016, he said, "Alice Randall is a foremother of transgressive feminist country. From the simple 'Small Towns (Are Smaller for Girls)' and 'God's a Woman,' to complex narratives like 'Girls Ride Horses, Too,' a woman running drugs and robbing dealers, including her man; 'The Ballad of Sally Anne,' a black bride holding a white community responsible for the lynching of her groom; or 'Reckless Night,' calling out church-based slut-shaming decades before the phrase was coined—she's told necessary untold stories, gotten them recorded, and into the charts."

I'm glad Odie's here to remember some of that, glad he's connecting some of the dots that don't always get connected. I want to do that for Lil.

People talk about country music starting in what was called the Big Bang in 1927, when Ralph Peer recorded the Carter Family and Jimmie Rodgers. I've always loved that Iris DeMent song "Mama's Opry," in which she tells the history, including the line "The Carters and Jimmie Rodgers played her favorite songs." Even the great Iris DeMent leaves out the part about Lil Hardin playing the piano for Jimmie Rodgers.

Motown, my town, Detroit City, was home for a period to the great black megastar Diana Ross, the extraordinary Gladys Knight, the incomparable Tammi Terrell, the devastatingly powerful Dinah Washington. None of these singers inspired me the way Lil did, precisely because she was so much more than a great singer.

Along the way Lil Hardin became a seamstress and a master tailor, a French teacher and a piano teacher—she did anything and everything that wasn't evil to keep on creating. She did it without the big stages, the big money, and the loud applause. But she did it. To her very end. She was unstoppable.

Lil Hardin died sitting on a piano bench. She was playing "St. Louis Blues," in honor of her ex-husband, Louis Armstrong, who had passed two months earlier. Lil died as she had lived: creating. I am learning how to be old from Lil Hardin.

There is a story that is completely the truth that hurts me so much it is impossible to speak of and hard to write. It is the story of how a woman in the business cheated me out of so much money getting me to sign a contract I hadn't read, which she assured me was the same as a previous contract. It wasn't. When I asked this lady about what she had done, she calmly explained, "It was my job to trick you if I could."

Lil had so many bad deals, people putting their names on her songs, but she kept on writing, kept on singing. She once said in an interview something to the effect of "I never was going to be a big star, but I always was a star, a little star, up there in the sky twinkling."

I like Lil's attitude. I like to think I am a little star. Bringing some light in the darkness. Reflecting the warmth of a distant sun. I am fifty-seven years old. Lil's been with me fifty-seven years. I don't have her ear or hands—but maybe I can put a few syllables together a little better than she could. I have just this year written my first song all by myself, words and music. The title is "Lil and Louis in L.A."

They rolled into town in a ca-di-llac car
Two righteous sidemen for a bright country star
And Lil said, that Rodgers boy knows a little sumptin
  'bout the blues
About being low and hungry with nothing left to lose
Lil and Louis in El-A
Louis gonna be a star some day

And Lil she's gonna be a star too
In a silk dress and a hat of blue
Lil and Louis in El-A
Making music every day
Lil and Louis in El-A
Making love their way

Lil wore a sharp silk dress and a trim blue hat
Her Mister Armstrong wore pleated pants and clean spats
And Jimmie said, that Lillian gal knows a little sumptin
  'bout the blues
About being sad and lonely with nothing left to lose
Lil and Louis in El-A
Making music every day
Lil and Louis in El-A
Making love their way

Lil slid 'cross the piano bench on Louis' loving hips

Louis eyeballed Jimmy's music put the horn to his lips
And soon it was Lil's brown fingers flying 'cross black
      and white keys
And Louis blowing sound kisses to Lil's sweet knees

July 19, 1931
If there's ten biggest days in music
That got to be one
The day Lil, Louis and Jimmy
Did Blue Yodel number nine
If I get to choose one that would be mine
Lil and Louis in El-A
Making music every day
Lil and Louis in El-A
Making love their way

Jimmy and Louis found fortune and fame
Nobody much remembers Lil Hardin's name
Like so many gals behind the music man
Her name got erased by the times of sand
Lil and Louis in El-A
Doing the country their way

Louis he got to be a great big star
Lil got to ride in his Cadillac car

My life in country has been the life of a little star, flashes here and there, songs in a movie, *The Thing Called Love*, song in a television show, *XXX's and OOO's*, writing a video of the year for Reba McEntire, publishing Garth, signing and publishing Mark Sanders. Working on Johnny Cash music videos. Making it into the number one club and into the ASCAP Silver Circle and becoming for a while a voting member of the CMA. Over twenty songs recorded. I've walked my share of red carpets.

That doesn't happen without Lil. But that isn't the greatest gift Lil gave me. The greatest gift was her push, by example, to focus on the creating, on doing the work, on telling the necessary stories, on the business as a part of self-ownership, on not being afraid of helping other people with their careers—the way she helped Jimmie Rodgers, the way she helped Louis Armstrong—regardless of whether or not they helped her, rather than focusing on visibility, fame, or simple acknowledgment.

Which brings me back to Lil in 1931, that period when Lil was in her early thirties and helping Jimmie Rodgers make country music history. Ray Charles was just being born, wasn't a year old. When Ray Charles would get into his early thirties he would record *Modern Sounds in Country and Western Music*. And you can bet he knew who played on "Blue Yodel #9." Ray Charles knew Lil and Ray Charles knew Louis.

When Willie Nelson and Buck Owens say that Ray Charles influenced them, I believe they are saying, without knowing they are saying, that Lil Hardin influenced them, too. And through Ray Charles, Lil was an influence on Solomon Burke and Van Morrison. *Modern Sounds in Country and Western Music* is my first favorite country album. I strongly suspect it was Lil's, too. And I suspect Lil played some role in the creation of that album that is not yet documented.

"Just for a Thrill" came out in 1959, throwing Lil Hardin Armstrong and Ray Charles into contact. In 1962 Ray Charles put out a country album. Lots of parts to that, but I suspect some small unrecognized part was Lil Hardin.

In 1978, seven years after Lil Hardin's death, Ringo Starr had a hit, "Bad Boy," with a Lil Hardin tune. It was a rewrite of Hardin's 1936 Decca Records tune "Brown Gal." For a brown gal who toted a Beatles lunch box to an all-black Motown kindergarten classroom, that's an inspiring thing: Lil taught me that our work lives on after us.

I too, am "just another brown girl all full of vim, chocolate gal, good intentions." And one of my intentions, which was also one of Lil's, was to put my fingerprints on country music, and another was to write songs.

"Struttin' with Some Barbecue" is one of my favorite Lil

Hardin compositions. It's also a song Louis Armstrong recorded and performed with frequency. As Lil originally wrote it, "Struttin' with Some Barbecue" was an instrumental tune. Every time I hear it, I think of Lil empowering generations of listeners. Show yourself, inhabit yourself, with pride. Be the barbecue and the strut. Go where you want to go into the heart of the country—and go well fed—and walk as Lil Hardin walked.

That's how I got to Memphis.

ele

WANDA JACKSON

———

When She Starts Eruptin'

HOLLY GEORGE-WARREN

Some people like to rock, some people like to roll
But movin' and a-groovin's gonna satisfy my soul
Let's have a party!

W hen I first heard those lines, snarled with a ferocious twang, backed by barrelhouse piano, I was a punk rocker with a penchant for hillbilly music. *Whoa!* I'd found my theme song. Recently relocated from North Carolina to New York's East Village, I spent my time checking out bands every night, scribbling reviews and waiting tables to keep me in beer and burgers. I can't remember if Wanda Jackson's "Let's Have a Party" grabbed me while I was tuned to a college radio station or listening to a friend's mixtape, but the effect was similar to that of another lyric I'd soon discover from Wanda's repertoire: "When I start eruptin' ain't nobody gonna make me stop!" (from "Fujiyama Mama"). I eventually found a used copy of the 1960 LP *Rockin' with Wanda!* at one of the numerous vinyl emporiums that dotted St. Mark's Place and Second Avenue. I was hooked!

In 1980, of course, resources were limited when it came to tracking down music and its makers: who was this woman with the "nasty" voice (as I later discovered her early press labeled her)? She had as much energy and in-your-face attitude as the postpunk bands I pogoed to night after night at CBGB, Max's Kansas City, and Hurrah.

I'd recently fallen for George Jones, Tammy Wynette, Loretta

Lynn, and the late Hank Williams and Patsy Cline. Which group was Wanda in, I wondered: was she dead or alive? There were few books on country & western or rock & roll history then; I consulted the handful that existed—including those produced by Rolling Stone Press, where I landed a day job in 1982—but found not a word about Wanda Jackson.

Wanda became a passion shared with my friend Nancy (a.k.a. Jim Shortz, whose fanzine *Short Newz* was one of my first writing platforms); we'd listen to her before slamming against each other at Bad Brains gigs at A7. Wanda's fiery version of "Riot in Cell Block #9" gave us the gusto to hold our own among the stage divers. And "Hot Dog! That Made Him Mad!," Wanda's ammunition for dealing with bad boyfriends, came in handy in those days. In the early to mid-eighties, rockabilly was in the air, but it was tame compared to the music of the feisty, ferocious Wanda.

Finally, while touring the South with Das Furlines, my all-girl punk rock/polka band, I met Lady Clare, a member of Atlanta's Now Explosion. Another rabid Wanda fan, she had the goods! She'd been collecting Wanda Jackson records for years and turned me on to her favorites, including 1960s country 45s and LPs and gospel discs from the seventies and eighties. Even in this more conservative milieu, Wanda did not refrain from putting across a song with badass attitude, as on the pedal steel–drenched "My Big Iron Skillet" (1969):

> *You are doing wrong again it's plain for all to see*
> *And you think here at home is where I ought to be*
> *There's gonna be some changes made when you get*
> *   in tonight*
> *Cause I'm gonna teach you wrong from right*
> *With my big iron skillet in my hand*
> *Gonna show you how a little woman can whip a great*
> *   big man*
> *If you live through the fight we're gonna have when*
> *   you get home*
> *You'll wake up and find yourself alone.*

Clare also turned me on to the Wanda track that became my all-time favorite: "Funnel of Love," a whirling, lusty number (who knew Roy Clark could play such slinky guitar?), which was the soundtrack to my developing relationship with drop-dead-gorgeous Robert Warren, then bassist with New York's Fleshtones but originally from Atlanta, and best friend since childhood of Clare's beau, Todd. Wanda worked in mysterious ways.

The year after Robert and I married, I finally got my hands on the first CD anthology of Wanda Jackson's lengthy career, Rhino's *Rockin' in the Country* (1990). Rich Kienzle's informative liner notes filled in some pieces to the puzzle: born in Oklahoma in October 1937 to an amateur musician and his seamstress wife, Wanda was primed from a young age to hit stages herself. She saw Rose Maddox, a major influence in sound and style, at the Riverside Rancho when the family moved to Los Angeles during World War II. (A few years ago, Wanda told me about seeing Maddox: "She was so feisty, so full of spunk, and they wore all those colorful, sparkly clothes. I said, 'I gotta be like her!'")

After their return to Oklahoma, Wanda got her own radio show at age thirteen, and began performing with Hank Thompson and others in Oklahoma City at fifteen. She scored a country & western hit in 1954 (a duet with Billy Gray), but it was after touring with Elvis Presley in 1955 and '56 that she started singing "hillbilly boogie," recording her first record for Capitol in 1956. She and Elvis had a thing, and he gave her a ring. Wanda's early records zigzagged between fledgling rock & roll and C&W; "I Gotta Know" showcased both sides of Jackson's repertoire in one song, with verses alternating between a slow country fiddle sound and an electric guitar-fueled raveup, and vocals seesawing easily between the two styles. The single hit number 15 on the C&W charts.

In 1956, there wasn't an abundance of rockabilly numbers told from a woman's point of view. So Wanda decided to write her own, beginning with the raucous "Mean Mean Man," in which her growl reaches new heights of female expression.

Buck Owens was among the Capitol session men who played on her early sides, but backing her live performances, beginning in 1958, was a Kansas City combo, Bobby Poe and the Po Kats, featuring the African American piano player Big Al Downing. Wanda broke the color and gender barriers as she toured the South with Big Al and the Po Kats. Influenced by Ray Charles, Little Richard, and Fats Domino, Downing's keys figured prominently in Wanda's 1958 recordings, as did the twin guitar leads played by Buck and Po Kat guitarist Vernon Sandusky. Downing and Sandusky also provided background vocals, as on the rollicking call to arms "Rock Your Baby," another of Wanda's early originals.

The combustible "Fujiyama Mama," a 1957 single, became a smash in Japan after it was picked up by Armed Forces Radio overseas. The music historian Colin Escott once wrote that on this song, "Wanda sang like a late summer Oklahoma tornado ripping through a trailer park." Wanda and company cut the explosive "Let's Have a Party" in 1958, but it didn't become a Top 40 hit until 1960, when it was discovered by a Des Moines DJ, who played it constantly. Through all her rock & roll successes, Wanda still loved country-tinged ballads, and several of her own early songs were written in that vein, including the torchy "Sinful Heart" (1958).

In the early 1960s, Roy Clark joined her new band, the Party-Timers, which she put together for a long string of bookings in Las Vegas. They rocked out on the defiant "Hard Headed Woman," with another killer guitar solo by Clark. One day, I would coproduce a Wanda Jackson tribute album by that name—but I'm getting ahead of myself!

In 1961, another original, the country weeper "Right or Wrong," yielded Wanda's second biggest hit (#9 on the country charts, #29 on the pop charts). For *Lovin' Country Style* (1962), she and her father, Tom Jackson, wrote the classic honky-tonk number "Wasted," which showcased some fine fiddle and pedal steel work.

Wanda always had an instinct for picking unique C&W material: for example, she was the first to record "Silver Threads and Golden Needles" (on her 1956 debut LP). Performed in 1962 by Janis Joplin and her bluegrass trio, the Waller Creek Boys, the song also became a hit for the Springfields (featuring Dusty Springfield) that year. Some of my favorites among Wanda's early country repertoire: the tear-jerkin' story song "Tennessee Women's Prison," Hank Cochran's "A Little Bitty Tear," and the fab "Cowboy Yodel," in which she yodeled up a storm (move over, Carolina Cotton!). She would display her thrilling yodel again in 2011 in her cover of Jimmie Rodgers's "Blue Yodel #6" (which she first recorded in 1966) on the Jack White–produced *The Party Ain't Over!*

In the seventies and eighties, Wanda seemed to disappear, but she was actually still performing. She and her devoted husband/manager, Wendell Goodman, became committed Christians in 1971, and Wanda focused on spiritual music, recording for Myrrh and other gospel labels and performing songs like "Jesus Put a Yodel in My Soul" and "I Saw the Light," mostly for church parishioners.

In 1985, Wanda began performing rockabilly in Scandinavia, Germany, and England to ecstatic audiences. A decade later, Texas-born, L.A.-based Rosie Flores, a talented guitarist/singer-songwriter and mover/shaker in the roots-rock scene that included Dwight Yoakam, the Blasters, and Los Lobos, sought out Wanda to sing on her *Rockabilly Filly* album. Thank you, Rosie Flores, because that's how I finally got to see Wanda Jackson in the flesh, at New York's Bottom Line in early 1996.

Wanda hit the stage that night in a bright white pantsuit shimmering with her trademark fringe. By then, I'd viewed bootleg videocassettes of her TV appearances in the fifties on *Ranch Party*, shaking her skintight go-go dresses while she played guitar and sang. At the Bottom Line, Wanda, then sixty and gorgeous with a big black bouffant 'do, still had that irresistible charisma as she growled "Rock Your Baby," "Hard-Headed

Woman," "Hot Dog!," "Fujiyama Mama," "Honey Bop!" and, of course, "Party." Jumping up and down and bopping along, I hung on to every word she sang. So many years after my initial obsession, there she was—looking and sounding amazing! I was hoarse by night's end from screaming, but that didn't stop me from rushing backstage to ask her to autograph my copy of *Rockin' with Wanda*, which she signed with the prophetic "Let's Rock On Forever!" I met the wonderful Wendell, and told them both about *Trouble Girls*, a book on the history of women in rock & roll that I was overseeing as editorial director of Rolling Stone Press. Of course, Wanda was included. I was producing a concert for the book's 1997 publication, featuring such legends as Ruth Brown and Ronnie Spector. Would Wanda consider performing too?

She was in!

Fast-forward to the following November, and my husband, Robert, led the New York Party-Timers backing Wanda at the Manhattan club Tramps. It was a night I'll never forget: Wanda representing rockabilly and country, alongside her aforementioned peers from girl groups, R&B, early rock & roll (Goldie & the Gingerbreads), and punk (Bush Tetras), and such singer-songwriters as Lucinda Williams, Victoria Williams, and Dar Williams. It seemed almost like a dream, watching sexy Wanda singing "Right or Wrong" directly to Robert onstage. She was flirting with my husband! That night, Wanda cast her spell on all the guys in the band; they were smitten with her and would accompany her several times over the next few years. Those musical assignations were magical, including one that took place at yet another book publication party, for a kids' book I wrote called *Shake, Rattle, and Roll: The Founders of Rock and Roll*, which featured Wanda.

Two months after the Tramps concert, I gave birth to our son, Jack, and guess who sent a beautiful flower arrangement? At seven weeks, Jack got to meet Wanda in person at her SXSW gig in Austin, and she's remained a presence in our lives ever since. During one of my first trips alone after becoming a mom, I spent a few days at Wanda and Wendell's home in Oklahoma City while researching a biography of Gene Autry. I was missing Jack and Robert, and Wanda commiserated, telling me how hard it was for her being away from her young son and daughter when she was playing her Las Vegas residency. Though her parents looked after their children back home, Wanda and Wendell eventually left Vegas to spend more time with them.

Of course, at her house, Wanda did everything she could to entertain me. She set up a tape player with a cassette of her dear friend Norma Jean (Porter Wagoner's early singing partner) by my bed in my lovely guest suite. She showed me her china cabinet filled with mementos from her many trips to Japan, let me strum her original girlhood guitar, and allowed me to thumb through the pages of her scrapbooks. We drove around town in her red convertible (with the top down, of course) while she sang along to a tape of her music. She took me to her favorite wine bar, and we spent an afternoon at the memorial for the victims of the Oklahoma City terrorist attack. There, she charmed a guard who approached us when we strolled through an area with a sign saying "Do Not Walk on Grass." After a few words with Wanda, rather than reprimand us, he took a photo of us together by one of the monuments. Wanda just has that way with people: when she breaks the rules, she's so sweet about it that you can't help but let her have her way. I guess that's what it took to knock down the doors to the boys' club back in the 1950s.

Since then, I've interviewed her numerous times for books, articles, liner notes, and oral history projects. Robert wrote her a fabulous song ("I Wore Elvis' Ring") that she cut on the 2006 album *I Remember Elvis*, plus he and the Party-Timers backed her for a 2003 live album, recorded in New York and titled *Still Alive and Kickin'*. Our little circle of Wanda fans has exploded big-time: Elvis Costello, the Cramps, Dave Alvin, and Justin Townes Earle are among the admirers who have recorded with her on *Heart Trouble* and *Unfinished Business*. A range of wonderful artists (among them Rosie Flores, Neko Case, Kelly Hogan, Kristi Rose, Jesse Dayton, and Robbie Fulks) contributed to the *Hard Headed Woman* tribute album I coproduced for Bloodshot. Adele personally chose Wanda to open her first big-time US tour. On his radio show, Bob Dylan called her "an atomic fireball of a lady." Over the past twenty years, I've seen her perform in more than a dozen states in venues running the gamut from a punk club in Tulsa to the venerable Public Hall in Cleveland, and at gigs ranging from a steamy day in Tennessee at Bonnaroo to *Late Night With David Letterman*, backed by Jack White and his band (who joined her on the acclaimed album *The Party Ain't Over*). Most exciting of all, I got to see Wanda inducted by Rosanne Cash into the Rock & Roll Hall of Fame in Cleveland in April 2009. I was honored to write an essay for the evening's program, which said, in part:

In 1958, when a gutsy, guitar-playing gal from Oklahoma belted out "Let's Have a Party," a mandate for new music, she was the rare woman among the rockabilly cats mixing up rhythm & blues and country & western, creating primal rock & roll in the process. Wanda Jackson wasn't afraid to step outside the prim confines of a woman's place in pop— sonically, lyrically, and aesthetically. She snarled, using a "nasty" voice to sing sassy lyrics, when "girl singers" were supposed to sound pretty and look pretty. Instead of going the cowgirl, country lass, or prom queen route, the gorgeous brunette dressed in befringed cocktail dresses that shimmied and shook as she cut the rug onstage. With her unique bluesy yelps and raucous growls, sensual and energized stage presence, and catchy, rhythmic repertoire, Jackson helped change the face of popular music. Today, 55 years after recording her first single, in 1954, Jackson is still rockin' on stages around the world.

These words hold true today . . .

As for the future: I'm planning a trip for myself to celebrate the completion of my biography of Janis Joplin (another artist influenced by Wanda) in early 2017. I'll be boppin' along with Wanda Jackson on the outrageous Outlaw Country Cruise— sailing the high seas with the Queen of Rockabilly, and the queen of my heart.

HAZEL DICKENS

The Plangent Bone

RONNI LUNDY

plan·gent
adjective/literary
(of a sound) loud, reverberating, and often melancholy.
synonyms: melancholy, mournful, plaintive

An editor wrote me recently to say, "What a splendid word!," and then confessed he'd had to look it up. How did I happen to know it, he wondered?

I don't remember ever needing to look the word up. The first time I read "plangent tone," I heard it in my body, maybe my soul. As I consider this, I place my hand at an angle across my chest, up from right below the heart to right beneath the shoulder. Here, I think. Here is where it lands. And if, like me, you were born in the Appalachian Mountains with family reaching back generations, then when a tone that's plangent sounds, something there trembles, then vibrates, deep to the bones. It's as if all us hillbilly children got an extra sinew, a plangent bone, a tuning fork to recognize the ancient tones.

Bill Monroe talked about and named them "ancient tones." He said they were one thing that distinguished his music, his bluegrass, from other forms of country song. He pushed those lamentations up out of his chest and sent them high and lonesome through his head, not just from his mouth, but seemingly through his very skull. They fall on listeners like electric shocks, making your hair stand on end, your ears tingle, and even, sometimes, your eyes weep tears.

Ralph Stanley sharpens those notes, pulls them from someplace even deeper, and when he sings, they grab you by the throat. Emmylou, she works some secret alchemy and sends them out on the wings of birds, feathers strumming a lute.

But the person who shapes and sends those notes from that very spot in her chest straight to the one in yours, bone to bone, soul to soul, is Hazel Dickens. If you wonder what I mean, go now, right now, to whatever device you have and call up "A Few More Years Shall Roll" by Hazel and Alice. The liner notes say Alice Gerrard is the lead and Hazel the tenor, but what I would say is that Hazel is the knife. The one that just ripped the curtains wide open.

———

Hazel Dickens was born near Bluefield, in Mercer County, West Virginia—right on the Virginia line, not that far from East Kentucky, in the heart of coal country. Her father was a Primitive Baptist preacher with a powerful singing voice. "I always sang, because we grew up that way," she said. They—Hazel and her ten siblings—also grew up poor, dependent on a fickle coal economy whose boom-and-bust cycles had played havoc with the land and people for generations. The economic slide of the early 1950s was just one of the many that had sent mountain folks elsewhere, often to the cities, looking for work. Hazel left for Baltimore, where some of her siblings already were, in 1951. She was sixteen years old.

Nineteen fifty-one was the same year my father packed us up in his truck and took us from family and home-places in and around Corbin, Kentucky, to Louisville, where the distilleries would provide him with work. I was almost two years old. My sister was nearly fourteen, closer to Hazel's age than mine, the both of them coming of age in a world very different from the one I would inhabit in my teens and twenties. The rebels, with and without a cause, of their generation were all young white boys with the privilege the world afforded them to sow wild oats. Girls and women, however, had their places and were expected to stay in them—such as the young wife of a good man, which my sister, a better writer than I, became at nineteen, putting aside her ambitions. Young waitress, sales clerk, and factory girl who sometimes got to play the bass in the boys' bluegrass band: those were Hazel's.

In the winter of 1969, the year I turned twenty, I dropped out of college for the first time and convinced my boyfriend to drive us to Florida because sun was what we needed. We returned after a very long weekend, I got a job, and I re-enrolled the next semester. And then dropped out again, and forayed out a little, and reeled back in again until, in the September of 1971, I retired from college permanently and my friend Cindy and I set out for Colorado in her old blue Valiant station wagon. That precipitated seven years of almost biblical wandering. I crisscrossed North America multiple times, in the Valiant, an old blue Pontiac, a salvaged mail delivery van, a VW station wagon, and my dad's '56 Chevy. I rode trains, buses, ferries, and a coastal postal boat around the edge of Newfoundland. I put 28,000 miles on my thumb. I made these trips with friends. I made them alone. Occasionally I made them with a stranger. It was a life my sister could not have imagined, that I hardly imagined as I was living it. It was the journey of discovery vouchsafed to men from *The Odyssey* to *On the Road*, but hardly ever given to women. Along the way I found pieces of myself I'd not known existed. Music was one of the glues I used to put those often disparate pieces together.

I've written before about how the old voices—Monroe's and Stanley's—reinforced for me the sense of connection to the older, rural world of my birth, my family, and my Appalachian heritage. And I've written even more about how one night, in a tiny club in Louisville, Kentucky, as I was sitting at the edge of a stage where a blond-haired god in overalls was ripping the strings off his fiddle playing Leon Russell's "Prince of Peace," the New Grass Revival finally helped me see how my past fit perfectly into the changing world that was my present. But I've not talked much, if ever, about what was still missing.

"Don't fall in love with me darling, I'm a rambler," Tony Rice would croon from the rinky-dink stage at the Holiday Inn in Lexington where we'd go to see J. D. Crowe. I'd grin and nod my head, knowing "the lure of the road," loving the faux-nobility of the "gotta go!" ("It's all for your sake, dear, that I'm leaving . . ."). Swimming in the song, I'd be, completely ignoring the fact that my part was to stay behind, to be "the sweetest sweetheart in the world . . ." Tony was a Freeborn Man, his home upon his back. I thought I was free, too, able to fit my life into a backpack. But the music told me otherwise. I was still a lady who, if I didn't mind my p's and q's, would be staring down the barrel of a shotgun filled with rock salt and nails.

Of course, this wasn't just—or even particularly—Tony's oeuvre. The bluegrass world was filled with instructions for women, the most somber being that if you fell in love with the wrong guy—and they were plentiful—he'd repay you for your love with brutal death. Maybe that scared me enough that despite my wandering ways, I also listened and worked hard to be the Linda Lou who could bring my rambling man back to old Kentucky, the gentle gal who kept his sleeping bag rolled up and stashed behind my couch, the good woman whose love could cure all that ailed him, on land and on sea. To be sure, if I wanted feminist road music, all I had to do was break out some Joni Mitchell. But how could *she* truly be my role model, the golden-haired goddess of Laurel Canyon who ruled the airwaves and stages and whom all the boys loved? I was a broke, plump, confused little Kentucky girl whose mother always ended each long-distance call by asking when I would finally come home. I could listen to Joni with admiration, but I was never going to be asked to sit at her lunch table.

And then a friend, a one-time traveling buddy, played "Hello Stranger" for me, sung by Hazel and Alice. "Get up rounder, let a working *girl* lay down," they sang, and I got that chill of recognition, and pride. Not from the plangent tone this time, but from the delicious possibility the song laid out. A life, perhaps lost, definitely hard, but surely independent and maybe as exciting as any offered to a man—but this time, the story belonged to a woman, sung in a woman's voice. Even now, the lines "weeping like a willow / and mourning like a dove . . ." will come to mind unbidden and, despite the contradiction of their melancholy import, make my heart leap at the idea of an adventure that is worth the cost.

The friend, let's call her Ann, was someone I'd gone to college with but had hardly known then. We'd lived in the same dorm my sophomore year and barely spoken. Four—or was it five?—years later I was waiting tables at a tourist restaurant at the end of the season in Bar Harbor, nursing a broken heart. One drizzly fall morning a young woman in hiking boots was sitting alone at my station. I recognized her, but could not place her for certain in any of the places I'd been: Colorado? New Mexico? California? Indiana? "Would you like coffee?" I asked, and when she grinned and said, "Yes, ma'am," I knew she was from Kentucky. Something plangent in that tone.

There's another story to be told about my friendship with Ann: one that involves trains, ferries, hitchhiking and that postal coastal boat, Joni Mitchell, a bucket of Kentucky Fried Chicken, and a night in a dance hall with sailors who spoke no English but insisted that we dance. It's not the story I'm telling now. The story I'm telling now came a couple of years after that one, after we'd reconnected, back in Kentucky. My heart had mended, and Ann was married to a boy she'd gone to school with, who kept asking her.

We had talked about him on our wild ride from Maine to Newfoundland. She continued from there by train across Canada, a trip she unequivocally called "the last thrill of my lifetime." She planned to go back to the small town in central Kentucky where this boy lived and marry him when the train ride ended. She was absolutely clear she did not love him, and doubted he really loved her, although he said he did. I, so full of romance and convinced love would find justice in the end—or vice versa—could not dissuade her from what I saw as a miserable and doomed path. "I want a farm," she said simply. "I've always wanted a farm. I'm a woman, and I'm not going to ever earn enough to buy one. He's got a farm. It's my only way."

It was at that farm that Ann sat me down on the floor in front of the stereo and played me both sides of both the records she owned by Hazel and Alice. I'd met the boy—now her husband—on his way out as I came in. He struck me as smug. As his truck door slammed, I asked if she was happy, and she shrugged. She swept her hand to the window and said, "Look at this. It's my farm," and then she fed me lamb that was a little bloody and coffee that was bitter, with evaporated milk. We took the coffee and sat in front of the stereo for almost two straight hours. We didn't talk much, only listened—except when Ann said of one song, "I really want you to pay attention to this one here."

> *You pull the strings*
> *she's your play thing*
> *you can make her or break her, it's true.*
> *You abuse her, accuse her, turn around and use her*
> *and forsake her anytime it suits you.*

"Don't Put Her Down, You Helped Put Her There" is a requiem for the life of a prostitute, but this is not the usual male-devised story of a violent end, or of the whore with a golden heart. And unlike the other feminist songs of that era—prideful anthems, or wry declarations of independence from a man who keeps doing the woman he's with wrong—"Don't Put Her Down" is about the systemic control and exploitation of women by men. It's about the "damned if you do, damned if you don't" choices that are a woman's life. It's about the price women must pay to simply survive. It's not one-dimensional in the way that polemics tend to be: in a few short verses it not only points a justified finger at the perpetrators but also touches on the complexities of compliance in a way that should break listeners' hearts while opening their minds.

She hangs around
playing the clown
while her soul is aching inside
she's heartbreak's child 'cause she just lives for your smile
to build her up in a world made by men.

When I listened to this song in the mid-1970s, sitting on my friend's floor, I took it as a rallying cry. Perhaps she did, too, since not that long after, she divorced that boy and found other ways to live her life. I believed I would live to see a time when its politics and poignancy would be quaint. Instead, I am dismayed at how many times over the next four decades it has come, unbidden, into my head because of its aptness. It could and should have been the anthem of the 2016 campaign season. It is a song that seems destined to last the ages.

The song is Hazel's, written by her and sung from both the hip and the heart; lived veracity is what gives it its power. Hazel called her move to the shipyard regions of Baltimore "a shock and an education." She said that music "was my lifeline. The only way I had of expressing myself, and I had a lot of stuff inside me to express." The city culture and its mores were alien to a preacher's daughter from the mountains. In many ways, the poverty was harsher, and the choices laid out for women, while perhaps more numerous, were no better—and arguably were worse—than those she'd had at home. Hazel chose the "good girl" route—waitress, shop clerk, factory worker—jobs that paid less than many others (and in which women were paid less than men performing the same work), but which were "respectable"—that is, if you agreed that a woman working at all was respectable, which was a question hotly debated at that time (and sometimes still is). But her respectability didn't keep her from seeing or speaking the truth about the lives of other women, and the poor.

"'Working Girl Blues' was written from a lot of strong feelings," Hazel wrote in the liner notes about another of her original songs. "Remembering and reliving all the bad jobs I've held from the time I was sixteen, the exploitation of working-class people and the unending cycle of shame it breeds. This song is written and dedicated to all working-class people."

These were my people she was singing for, defined and curtailed by class and culture. This was me she was singing for, defined and denied by gender. She did so with a precision that cut away all the rationalizations offered by the privileged. She also did so with a deep streak of rebellion, one that offered other options.

"There's a whole lot of places / my eyes are longing to see / where there is no green cottage / no babies on my knee / and there's a lot of people / just waiting to shake my hand," she offers, the antidote to all those rambling boys, in "Ramblin' Woman."

Hazel Dickens dedicated most of her life and work to the stories of the people who make up what we euphemistically—and somewhat wistfully—call the working class. What we mean is people who work or don't work at the whim of the privileged, those who call the shots about the conditions of that work and reap the largest benefits from it.

She sang abundantly—in both her songs and others'—about the lives of coal miners and their families: "Coal Tattoo," "Mining Camp Blues," "They'll Never Keep Us Down." She gave voice to the voiceless, writing "Black Lung" for the brother who stayed home and worked down in the mines all of his life—and died, she noted, without enough money to pay for his burial. "That should never happen," she said.

We live in an era in which celebrities contribute their time and voices to benefits for many causes, performing in studios or arenas far removed from any danger. But Hazel went into the heart of the battle, singing at union rallies, singing for the miners, their spouses, and their children who sat in the audience and heard their lives acknowledged. She sang for the strikers protesting Pittson Coal's arbitrary and brutal discontinuation of health benefits. She was the soundtrack for the documentary covering the Brookside strike, "Harlan County, U.S.A." Google "Hazel Dickens" and "Upper Big Branch" and you will see that even though she didn't sing about it directly, she is the voice of the thirty-eight miners killed in that blast, the voice calling for justice from the Don Blankenships of the world who own the mines, and who decide the fates of the miners with negligence and impunity. Hers has become the voice of countless miners' wives and children, crying out from the graveyards. Hers the plangent voice from deep within the mountain that contains their bones and souls.

> *How can god forgive you*
> *You know what you done.*
> *You killed my husband*
> *now you want my son.*

"Loretta Lynn is the coal miner's daughter, Hazel Dickens is the coal miner's heroine," wrote a fan not long ago on a YouTube post. If you do not understand the risk involved in Dickens's choice to not just sing about but to *be* about resistance in mining country, then call up "The Yablonski Murder" on YouTube. *"Well, it's cold-blooded murder, friends, I'm talking about . . ."* Hazel wrote the song in 1970, when she learned of the bloody assassination of union organizer Joe "Jock" Yablonski, his wife, and his daughter on New Year's Eve. Or rewatch John Sayles's *Matewan* (in which Hazel has a part) and understand that the story it tells isn't fiction but fact, about the spark that ignited the Battle of Blair Mountain, a battle in which rebellious miners, their wives and children, and other sympathizers were violently quelled by company thugs with the help of the US army.

Or, to better understand Hazel Dickens and her continuing impact, you could track down Mimi Pickering's film biography from Appalshop, *Hazel Dickens: It's Hard to Tell the Singer from the Song*. Cutting back and forth between images of grief and protest, Mimi's masterful work vividly shows Hazel and her music in the context of the lives she gives voice to, as well as placing her in an artistic context, with interviews from a diverse range of peers: Alison Krauss, Dudley Connell, Naomi Judd.

When Mimi's film came out, in 2001, I felt a vicarious pride tinged with just a bit of bittersweetness. Like most music writers, I have a small list of the people I long to write with, not just about. I call this the Biography List. It's the one a writer keeps because she feels a profound kinship with or connection to the singers and the songs, and believes that in writing about/with those people, she might come to know and better understand herself.

Mimi Pickering's amazing film didn't erase Hazel Dickens from my list. After all, a movie is not a book. And I continued for a long time to believe that "someday" I'd get to have the many and deep conversations with Hazel that her music and life prompted me to desire. But the news one April morning in 2011 ended that fantasy. At the age of seventy-five, Hazel Dickens had died. I felt the plangent bone in my chest begin to quiver.

And so I turned, as many have, to a voice to give voice to my grief. I found Hazel singing "Pretty Bird," a cappella, and as it began to play, the ache in my chest deepened.

> *Fly far beyond the dark mountain*
> *to where you'll be free evermore*
> *fly away little pretty bird*
> *where the cold winter winds don't blow.*

JUNE CARTER CASH

Eulogy for a Mother

ROSANNE CASH

Many years ago, I was sitting with June in the living room at home, and the phone rang. She picked it up and started talking to someone, and after several minutes I wandered off to another room, as it seemed she was deep in conversation. I came back ten or fifteen minutes later, and she was still completely engrossed. I was sitting in the kitchen when she finally hung up, a good twenty minutes later. She had a big smile on her face, and she said, "I just had the nicest conversation," and she started telling me about the other woman's life, her children, that she had just lost her father, where she lived, and on and on . . . I said, "Well, June, who was it?" and she said, "Why, honey, it was a wrong number."

That was June. In her eyes, there were two kinds of people in the world: those she knew and loved, and those she didn't know and loved. She looked for the best in everyone; it was a way of life for her. If you pointed out that a particular person was perhaps not wholly deserving of her love, and might in fact be somewhat of a lout, she would say, "Well, honey, we just have to lift him up." She was forever lifting people up. It took me a long time to understand that what she did when she lifted you up was to mirror the very best parts of you back to yourself. She was like a spiritual detective: she saw into all your dark corners and deep recesses, saw your potential and your possible future, and the gifts you didn't even know you possessed, and she "lifted them up" for you to see. She did it for all of us, daily, continuously. But her great mission and passion was lifting up my dad. If being a wife were a corporation, June would have been the CEO. It was her most treasured role. She began every day by saying, "What can I do for you, John?" Her love filled up every room he was in, lightened every park he walked, and her devotion created a sacred, exhilarating place for them to live out their married life. When June died, my daddy lost his dearest companion, his musical counterpart, his soul mate and best friend.

The relationship between stepmother and children is by definition complicated, but June eliminated confusion by banning the words "stepchild" and "stepmother" from her vocabulary, and from ours. When she married my father, in 1968, she brought with her two daughters, Carlene and Rosie. My dad brought with him four daughters: Kathy, Cindy, Tara, and me. Together they had a son, John Carter. But she always said, "I have seven children." She was unequivocal about it. I know, in the real time of the heart, that this is a difficult trick to pull off, but she was unwavering. She held it as an ideal, and it was a matter of great honor to her.

When I was a young girl at a difficult time, confused and depressed, with no idea of how my life would unfold, she held a picture for me of my adult life: a vision of joy and power and elegance that I could grow into. She did not give birth to me, but she helped me give birth to my future. Recently, a friend was talking to her about the historical significance of the Carter Family, and her remarkable place in the lexicon of American music. He asked her what she thought her legacy would be. She said softly, "Oh, I was just a mother."

June gave us so many gifts, some directly, some by example. She was so kind, so charming, and so funny. She made up crazy words that somehow everyone understood. She carried songs in her body the way other people carry red blood cells—she had thousands of them at her immediate disposal; she could recall to the last detail every word and note; and she shared them spontaneously. She loved a particular shade of blue so much that she named it after herself: "June-blue." She loved flowers and always had them around her. In fact, I don't ever recall seeing her in a room without flowers: not a dressing room, a hotel room, certainly not her home. It seemed as if flowers sprouted wherever she walked. John Carter suggested that the last line of her obituary read: "In lieu of donations, send flowers." We put it in. We thought she would get a kick out of that.

She treasured her friends and fawned over them. She made a great, silly girlfriend who would advise you about men and take you shopping and do comparative tastings of cheesecake. She made a lovely surrogate mother to all the sundry musicians who came to her with their craziness and heartaches. She called them her babies. She loved family and home fiercely. She inspired decades of unwavering loyalty in [companion and caretaker] Peggy and her staff. She never sulked, was never rude, and went out of her way to make you feel at home. She had tremendous dignity and grace. I never heard her use coarse language or even raise her voice. She treated the cashier at the supermarket in the same friendly way in which she treated the president of the United States.

I have many, many cherished images of her. I can see her cooing to her beloved hummingbirds on the terrace at Cinnamon Hill in Jamaica, and those hummingbirds would come, unbelievably, and hang suspended a few inches in front of her face to listen to her sing to them. I can see her lying flat on her back on the floor and laughing as she let her little granddaughters brush her hair out all around her head. I can see her come into a room with her hands held out, a ring on every finger, and say to the girls, "Pick one!" I can see her dancing with her leg out sideways and her fist thrust forward, or cradling her autoharp, or working in her gardens.

But the memory I hold most dear is of her two summers ago [in 2001] on her birthday in Virginia. Dad had orchestrated a reunion and called it Grandchildren's Week. The whole week was in honor of June. Every day, the grandchildren read tributes to her, and we played songs for her and did crazy things to amuse her. One day, she sent all of us children and grandchildren out on canoes, with her Virginia relations steering us down the Holston River. It was a gorgeous, magical day. Some of the more urban members of the family had never even been in a canoe. We drifted for a couple of hours, and as we rounded the last bend in the river to the place where we would dock, there was June, standing on the shore in the little clearing between the trees. She had gone ahead in a car to surprise us and welcome us as the end of the journey. She was wearing one of her big flowered hats and a long white skirt, and she was waving her scarf and calling, "Helloooo!" I have never seen her so happy.

So, today, a bereft husband, seven grieving children, sixteen grandchildren, and three great-grandchildren wave to her from *this* shore as she drifts out of our lives. What a legacy she leaves; what a mother she was. I know she has gone ahead of us to the farside bank. I have faith that when we all round the last bend in the river, she will be standing there on the shore in her big flowered hat and long white skirt, under a June-blue sky, waving her scarf to greet us.

May 18, 2003
Hendersonville, Tennessee

BRENDA LEE

Rare Peer

A tribute written by
TAYLOR SWIFT
when she was
fifteen years old

I'm curled up in my mother's bed, staring intently at my laptop. I'm watching a video of a familiar-looking man wearing a black tuxedo. The video seems to be of a televised award show. The tape is grainy, but the man steps up to the mic and his words are clear:

> Now I'm gonna deal you a queen from the winning hand. Her voice is full like solid gold, with some platinum blended in. Sometimes you'll hear silver when she twists and twirls her notes . . . but gold is Brenda's metal in this song I wish I'd wrote. Ladies and gentlemen . . . Brenda Lee.

The camera then focuses on a woman in her late thirties. The music starts, and she's looking down at a framed picture. She's at ease. She is theatrical. And she is beautiful, in a sparkling gown that matches the twinkle in her eye. Lights, camera, action. She starts to sing. That's when you hear the gold, and you watch her as she holds the crowd in the palm of her hand. The performance ends, and the crowd goes wild. The lovely lady graciously takes a bow. She smiles out into the vast darkness, taking it all in with grace and composure. The video ends, and I reflect back on what I just saw. It was a timeless performance, but here are the facts: The year is 1983. The song is "Someone Loves You Honey." The man in the tuxedo is Johnny Cash. And the woman in the beautiful dress with the honey-like voice is none other than Brenda Lee.

Brenda Lee, who was born in 1944 near Atlanta and used her prodigious singing talent to support her family after the tragic death of her father. Brenda Lee, the little girl who took over the music world with chart-topping hits when she was still a child. Brenda Lee, the woman who ushered in a new style of rock & roll and was one of the early musical artists to find her fame through television. Brenda Lee, the artist who later went back to her country roots, proving that she could create classics and break down barriers no matter what genre or category her music fell under. Brenda Lee, the singer who mastered the sound of heartbreak so flawlessly that she made audiences not only identify with her but believe her.

I watch the look on her face as she ends her song and first hears that applause. There's a reason she's been able to move people to their feet for almost sixty years. Brenda Lee is grace. Brenda Lee is class and composure. And when she hears the roar of a crowd, Brenda Lee smiles like she's five years old and receiving her first standing ovation. Brenda Lee is someone I will always look up to because of the way she shines. As Johnny Cash said in 1983, it's almost like she's *golden*.

BOBBIE GENTRY

Let the Mystery Be

MEREDITH OCHS

I t bleeds into you from the first bar and winds its way around your bones like a creeping vine. The guitar strums seventh chords, just one note off a standard major chord but enough to hint at a minor key elegy. Then the voice, gently seductive, lightly scratched by dust and hay, draws you to the humid Mississippi Delta. You imagine hands roughened by field work, the scent of magnolia in the air, and biscuits baking as dinner is readied in the modest house nearby. The song wastes no time; before the first verse is done painting this southern gothic scene, someone has committed suicide.

By the time I heard Bobbie Gentry sing "Ode to Billy Joe," it was already a staple on oldies radio stations—good ole terrestrial radio with its grandiose male announcers and wanting audio quality—in the New York metropolitan area, where I was raised. Even through a crackling speaker, the song felt so intimate that I sensed I already knew it—perhaps I'd heard it on the radio as a baby and it stayed in my veins. I can't pinpoint the first time I heard Gentry, but I remember holding my cheap cassette recorder up to my parents' stereo and taping "Ode to Billy Joe." It was the quickest way I, with no disposable income and no YouTube, could possess it. I played it, hit rewind, and played it again, over and over. Its mystery grew each time. Why did Billy Joe kill himself? Was the singer involved with him? What did they throw off the Tallahatchie Bridge? Southerners understand how everyone can discuss these kinds of events calmly over supper, but if you grew up in a family that debated things like politics and religion at the kitchen table, as I did, it boggled the mind.

"Ode to Billy Joe" wasn't Bobbie Gentry's only song, but it was her biggest hit, spending four weeks at number one on the *Billboard* Hot 100 when it was released in 1967. The B-side of the swamp-rocking "Mississippi Delta," which her record label, Capitol, thought would be the hit, it won four Grammys, three for Gentry herself. Both the single and the album knocked the Beatles out of the number-one spot on the charts.

The cryptic hit parallels the enigma of Gentry, who walked away from worldwide renown into total obscurity. She recorded seven albums and numerous singles, made many television appearances, hosted her own variety show for the BBC and CBS—*The Bobbie Gentry Happiness Hour*—and performed in Vegas. She last turned up on a Bob Hope Mother's Day special in 1981, then quietly slipped out of the limelight.

Gentry's personal life is also somewhat shrouded. The basic contours, we know: Roberta Lee Streeter grew up on her grandparents' farm in Chickasaw County, Mississippi, but moved to Southern California at thirteen to be with her mother. A stunning brunette, she worked as a model and a showgirl. She attended the Los Angeles Conservatory and UCLA and studied music and philosophy. She was a warm, engaging performer but an intensely private person. She was married three times, each time for no more than a year. She demonstrated her business acumen by, among other things, buying into the Phoenix Suns as a part owner.

Most importantly, Gentry was wildly creative and driven at a time when the music industry did not see artists in the roles of songwriter, producer, or visionary—particularly women artists. From the accounts of her colleagues, we know that she was not given proper credit for her music or her forays into television. It stands to reason that someone who laid down such lyrical melodies would hear fully realized songs in her head, and that someone who wrote with such a powerful visual sense would envision a TV show. She was a sophisticate who was fluent in rural ways because she had lived both lives, fostering her innate gifts with education and her own experiences.

If a country girl could become a cosmopolitan artist, then southern culture could resonate with one from the 'burbs. Growing up, I viewed this sort of duality as a roadblock. I couldn't reconcile my home life with my interests, all of which lay far beyond my domain. The feeling of not fitting in leads one on a search for answers to everything. The more I learned of Gentry, the more I realized that duality is the beginning of art, the beginning of adulthood.

But when I was a tween, no one in my life could explain "Ode to Billy Joe" to me, much less the rest of Bobbie Gentry's oeuvre. Not my parents, brainy first-generation Americans out of Brooklyn who were weathering the ice storm of the 1970s and the snowstorm of the 1980s. Not my friends, nor my teachers, nor my glamorous godmother, a radiant blonde Pan Am flight attendant who traveled the globe and brought pieces of it back to me in the form of gifts. Not even the sweet, clear-skinned collegian who came to my house every Monday afternoon and taught me to play folk songs on my girl-sized nylon-string acoustic guitar. I lived about as far from Choctaw Ridge as one could, and that's why Bobbie Gentry held such a fascination for me. She invited me into this inscrutable place and whispered to me of its secrets. I'd been to the Middle East, but not to Mississippi—in my own country! To me, Yazoo seemed more exotic than Fez.

Some children learn to compartmentalize their secrets and their dreams. My world was contained in a soulless suburb on the fringes of the city my parents had loved but abandoned in its time of ferment. But then there was this otherworld, accessible through the speaker of my radio. When Bobbie Gentry's songs played, I slid through a kudzu-draped portal into a South that I'd soon delve into more extensively via William Faulkner, Eudora Welty, Harper Lee, Flannery O'Connor, and many others, and later on through blues and country music. John Fogerty wrote songs about the bayou without ever having been there. I figured I could at least visit these places in my mind.

Bobbie Gentry's literate portraits of the South still live within me, but as I slowly acquired her catalog on vinyl, it was her songs about relationships that dug even deeper into my consciousness. In 1990, Reba McEntire had a hit with a mild-mannered version of Gentry's second-biggest single, "Fancy," and of course I needed to find the original. Vinyl records could be had cheaply in that decade. No one wanted the stuff; people would leave boxes crammed full of albums on the curb, where I'd carefully pick through them and pull the good ones, like *Fancy* (which was also the title of the album the song was on).

The tale of a mother who, out of poverty and desperation, tricks out her young daughter at a New Orleans brothel, "Fancy" was shocking at the time and now seems regressive. When it was released, the pro-ERA, pro–equal pay, pro-choice Gentry called it her "strongest statement for women's lib." But this mother-daughter dynamic caught my attention as being the polar opposite of the one in "Ode to Billy Joe." Fancy's mother has nothing to give her but empowerment, and as a result, Fancy changes her circumstances and climbs out of poverty. On the other hand, the gossipy, obfuscating mother in "Ode to Billy Joe" descends into an almost catatonic state at the song's end, becoming dependent on her daughter, whose life remains exactly the same. So "Fancy" isn't just a feminist anthem—it's also a lesson in what's important to impart to your children. For those of us who never narrowed the chasm between our mothers and ourselves that developed when we clicked into our teens, it's enlightening.

If "Ode to Billy Joe" is a snapshot of Gentry's childhood, "Fancy" is a metaphor for what followed, as she went from barefoot in the Delta to educated Angeleno to great success. Maybe it was a commentary on the way the music industry prostitutes its artists, specifically women. Apparently Gentry didn't care for the show part of show business, one of the reasons she may have ducked out of the public eye. Even in absentia, though, her achievements are reflected in the work of contemporary singer/songwriters: from the deep introspection and honeyed altos of Rosanne Cash and Allison Moorer, to the steadfast unconventionality of Neko Case, to the uncompromising way Lucinda Williams stuck to her vision in *Car Wheels on a Gravel Road* until it was flawless—and so many more.

The eternal mystery of Gentry and her songs is something that makes mystery itself acceptable to me. I spent a chunk of my adulthood as a seeker, an itinerant, sometimes a journalist, always trying to answer deep-seated questions. Why are we here, how did we arrive, what is our purpose, what can we believe in, what is moral, what is right? Navigating the minefield of work, love, and family relationships often ends with a painful "Why?" Someone leaves, someone returns, someone dies. How long do you shout into the void before accepting that there may be no answer, or before you realize that you've ended up back where you started, in one way or another? A very smart friend of mine who grew up in North Carolina told me a childhood story about the time he tagged along behind his grandfather, asking "Why?" about everything. Finally the exasperated old man spun around, stuck his grizzled face in the boy's face, and snapped, "There ain't no why!"

And sometimes, there ain't. Bobbie Gentry didn't just disappear after writing an American classic. She worked for a decade after she released her final solo album. But when she gave it up, she went dark. Perhaps she was frustrated with an industry that clung to its rampant sexism as the world around it struggled to change. Or perhaps she was tired of being misquoted and misrepresented; anyone who has ever been the subject of an interview knows it may not turn out to be a true representation of what you've said and what you stand for. Maybe she never repeated the success of "Ode to Billy Joe" because she won the cursed Best New Artist Grammy. Does she still write songs? Maybe people only have so many songs in them. Maybe she was just done with the whole thing.

You can spend your life searching for answers only to end up in the same place, and thanks to Bobbie Gentry I'm ok with that. Her legacy is far more significant than where she has been for the last thirty-five years, or why she left. Let the mystery be.

ello

LORETTA LYNN

The Pill

MADISON VAIN

Imagine a world where Loretta Lynn songs always existed. Such is my privilege.

Inarguably, Loretta Lynn is the greatest female singer to ever come out of Nashville. She's country music's sequined Queen of the Sexual Revolution and the sweetest voice to ever shout, "I know how you feel!" to generations of unheard and under-represented women. Since her 1963 debut, she has been the most human, and humorous, of paragons, speaking directly to the female rebel spirit—giving thousands of women the permission to insist to their men that if they can't treat them right, they better get used to treating them as gone. She's told us it's perfectly acceptable to not want another baby, and that if they want to file for divorce, it's just as well.

Of course, all of this was established long before I was born, in the fall of 1989. When I arrived in Town and Country, Missouri, on September 16 of that year, many of the feminist movement's battles, proclaimed in her lyrics, had been won: birth control was legal, leaving a cheating husband was respectable (and even better, a cheating man was deplorable), and admitting to "faking it" was, well, inevitable.

It's funny—in that perfectly unfunny way in which you recall the beautiful innocence you once possessed and are equal parts embarrassed and envious of your old vantage point—that I distinctly remember thinking "The Pill" was irrelevant when I first heard about it in history class. (Yes, by the time I entered high school, Loretta Lynn was a name heard in history class, in the section devoted to the women's liberation movement.)

It was 2003, my iPod was filled with the punkish southern rock of Kings of Leon and My Morning Jacket, and my teacher wanted me to believe "The Pill" was revolutionary. I'd been on birth control since I was twelve or thirteen years old. My dermatologist gave it to me to spare me the threat of adolescent acne. Both my sisters were on it. My mother was on it! Plus, Loretta Lynn had played on our classic country radio station my whole life—where was the riot? It was all deliciously lost on me.

Less than a year later, Loretta Lynn released *Van Lear Rose*, her collaborative album with Jack White. As I'd been swearing to my father for two years at that point, the White Stripes' *White Blood Cells* changed my life. I had an insatiable desire for anything Jack White touched—disclaimer: I still do—and as a result I began my dive into Loretta Lynn's music.

Rock critics wrote that year that White was introducing the country legend to an entire new generation of fans, and I was a perfect example. After *Van Lear Rose*, which was one of the first records I uploaded into that newfangled thing called iTunes, I worked through all the CDs my dad had shelved in his case. *Honky Tonk Angels*, which Loretta recorded with Dolly Parton and Tammy Wynette, was a particular favorite, as was her first greatest hits collection. I was obsessed, sure, but more than that, I was spoken to.

During my junior year in high school, I remember listening to "Wings Upon Your Horns" in my bedroom, headphones on and late at night, after I'd gotten serious with my first boyfriend and was mulling over his pleas to go all the way. I remember driving along to "You Ain't Woman Enough (To Take My Man)," imagining I was singing it out loud to my classmate Maggie, who was crossing a few too many lines for my liking. That next spring, after what I now know to be a particularly inconsequential breakup, I found myself being self-indulgent enough to sob to "I Miss Being Mrs. Tonight," a song so completely knowing about grief that it devastates me without fail even after hundreds of trips through it.

I'm still equal parts embarrassed and envious to tell you that while I'd found a refuge in Loretta Lynn, and even in some ways found myself, I still hadn't found the world. The revolution was still lost on me. And while I also wish I could say that it crashed down on me in dramatic, biblical fashion one fateful day in the early oughts—that something happened that set my vision right—it simply hasn't worked that way.

My dawning has been gradual.

You see, I was raised in a privileged, primarily white town in a privileged, primarily white suburb. I went to a private school that cost more than I, now working for a journalist's salary, can even believe. It was an all-girls school and was primarily staffed by female teachers. In short, I realize that the first eighteen years of my life were spent in an incredibly safe space, given the extremely vocal and ridiculously opinionated young woman that I am. I didn't break down boundaries of gender norms or expectations in my youth, nor was I ever forced to stand strong against the grain. I thrived, because I was nurtured to thrive.

I attended Wake Forest University in Winston-Salem, North Carolina. Wake Forest is a hard school, with a notoriously heavy workload. I remember lamenting this fact with a handful of my guy friends in the cafeteria one afternoon during the fall of my freshman year. I expected sympathy. Instead, one of them asked why I bothered at all. "If I were a pretty girl," he said, "I would just marry well. Someone from the business school." I think I was supposed to feel complimented that he found me attractive.

I didn't have a response to him then, and I still don't. Sometimes, when I see him at reunions or weddings, I wonder if he remembers saying it. Indeed, I wonder if he still thinks that way.

Leaving the dining hall that day, I thought about a conversation I'd had with my grandmother before setting off for school.

With tears in her eyes, she told me she was jealous of me. The world was so big for her granddaughters. When she was eighteen, she recalled, her choices were: become a nurse, become a secretary, become a mom. (That you would become a wife was implied, I suppose.) She was jealous because I could become any of those or none of those.

When she said it, I assumed my grandmother's times were past. My conversation with my classmate made me realize that there were men out there, otherwise kind and wonderful men, who didn't understand why women didn't envy the housewives of the fifties. They didn't understand female ambition. "The Pill" began to make more sense. I was sad that it did.

My first job out of college was at *Sports Illustrated* in New York City. I'd moved to Manhattan nearly six weeks before, with wide eyes and absolutely no plan of attack in terms of seeking employment. I sent a lot of "cold-call" e-mails and just as many follow-up e-mails, and spent every day extremely over-caffeinated from taking any writers I could find out for coffee to "pick their brains"—a.k.a., ask for a job.

Eventually I found Terry McDonell. As the managing editor of *SI*, he had minimal incentive to take a meeting with me, a twenty-two-year-old unemployed-but-hopeful reporter. We had a mutual connection who was kind enough to call in a favor, so with the stern warning that he didn't have a job available for me and that this was an informative interview only, Terry invited me to his midtown office.

For an hour that afternoon, Terry asked me who my favorite writers were, what movies made me cry, and what books were most dear to me. He didn't care whether I was proficient in Excel or a master of Microsoft Word. He asked what music stirred my soul. I think we may even have discussed whether I believe in souls.

Perhaps your parents at one time or another have mentioned that you should never believe someone who says they don't have a position available, and that there is always a job to be found or had in any office. I am here to say that I agree with them, and to serve as an example. I still don't know if Terry agreed with my answers or just liked that I had answers, but he hired me on the spot as his assistant. For the next six months we worked on editor's letters, layouts, brand extensions, and more. He let me sit in on meetings and afterward asked me what I thought. Occasionally, he liked what I thought enough to actually implement something around an idea of mine.

Unfortunately, Terry left *Sports Illustrated* and the Time Inc. family after that half year together. (He had been there for the previous eleven.) I floated through a few departments trying to find a more permanent home, and eventually had a meeting with management about where they saw me fitting in. "We thought you might like to join the *SI* swimsuit team," they suggested. I did, but my stint there was short, and for the next year I continued bouncing around, even to an independent PR firm for a bit, before settling at *Entertainment Weekly*.

I'm now a rock journalist, and although it's my dream field, it also has the stale air of an old boys' club. There have been artists, managers, and publicists who have squirmed when I offer my opinion. Three weeks ago, my boyfriend's close friend, who works in finance, told me I should consider sending him my articles before publishing them. He could "offer context," he said. I have been called "sweetie" more times than I can count, and a few in the industry have allowed themselves curiously wandering hands when they're near me. One time, a fellow concertgoer asked me why I was writing in my diary during a show.

"The Pill" makes perfect sense now. It's about having options and keeping them open.

At twenty-seven years old, I no longer see my inability to grasp the earth-shattering, -shaking, -shaping aspects of Loretta Lynn's music as a weakness of my youth. Rather, I see it as one of the defining strengths of her canon. That so much of her catalog can be both totally relevant to the movements of the sixties and seventies and irrevocably timeless is why so many continue to find themselves in her music, from Carrie Underwood, who brought "You're Looking at Country" back to the Opry stage, to

Paramore, who covered "You Ain't Woman Enough" on tour, to Jack White, who took on "Coal Miner's Daughter" as he chaired Record Store Day, to me: a completely average teenage girl from the Midwest singing in the car at the top of her lungs, windows down and hair whipping freely.

In some ways, even Lynn is part of that group now. Early in 2016, she released *Full Circle*, an excellent collection that sees the eighty-four-year-old taking stock of her tenure. She revisits favorite cuts from early in her career, like "Whispering Sea," and then goes even further, sharing folk standards that she sang with her mother during a rustic youth in Butcher Holler, Kentucky.

Before *Circle* released, I spoke with her for an article that would run in *Entertainment Weekly*. In the days prior, I'd prepared questions about specific songs and lyrics, about working with John Carter Cash, and about going back into the studio for the first time in a decade.

She told me about how her mommy would sing "Into the Pines" to her when she was little, but only if she promised to quit her crying. About how it makes her sad that her hometown recently got its first asphalt road: "I waded mud out of that Holler to my knees," she told me. "Everybody else ought to have to, too."

We talked about how she didn't see her daddy in the eight years leading up to his death in 1959, and how she wishes her seventy-six-year-old brother, Herman Webb, would charge more for the tours he gives of her childhood schoolroom to fans. We talked a lot about Kentucky and how it's hard for her to go back. "It left me," she said more than once. "I didn't leave it." She sang to me twice, old hill songs, and told me she was worried about Merle, referring to the now-late legend Merle Haggard, who was then still in the hospital.

Not as quickly as I would have liked, it occurred to me that I was helping compile a capsule memory of an America that will never be again. Considering the broad scope of what might perish with our indefatigable icon when the time comes, I wondered out loud if she felt a sense of duty to preserve Appalachian music. "That's true," she said, as simply as she has ever said anything.

Of course, Loretta Lynn's mortality had already occurred to Loretta Lynn. "Who's Gonna Miss Me?," the first single off *Circle*, ponders exactly what its title suggests. Listening to it now, I'm reduced to a puddle thinking she somehow doesn't know the answer: *Everyone who has ever heard you*. Everyone, but especially every woman who has, like myself, found a friend in her music, in that angelic voice that whispers the realest of realities into your ear, offering wisdom that you never anticipated needing but absolutely do.

Speaking with Loretta about what it was like to be the spark plug in any room made me think about my mother. Invariably, now, whenever I listen to any of Loretta's music, which is often, I still think of my mother and her pluck. I wonder if her gumption felt out of place in suburban Missouri in the 1960s. I chew on the possibility that if Loretta Lynn hadn't spoken up, my mother might have been quieted, ignored—dulled. My mother is effervescent. No matter the room, her aura fills it. But what if she wasn't allowed to be? Would my sisters and myself have then, in turn, been taught to bite our (admittedly sharp) tongues? Would we have been saddled with a universe of gray?

It's a rabbit hole I've found myself tumbling down frequently, forced to confront the twin pillars of misogyny and feminism. And when it all becomes too much, it's then that I remember my good fortune: I live in a world where Loretta Lynn songs have always existed.

If only everyone could say the same.

∼ele∼

DOLLY PARTON

———

Long Island Down Home Blues

NANCY HARRISON

I came to country music relatively late in life. Growing up in a suburb of Manhattan during the 1970s and 1980s, I was weaned on a steady diet of teenybopper pop. Shaun Cassidy and Leif Garrett were my prepubescent appetizers (yes, my room was wallpapered with their posters) before I began indulging in heftier fare, like Squeeze and U2.

My parents were a bit old-fashioned. My dad favored jazz and classical music, and my mom was all about Barbra Streisand and show tunes. If I wanted to explore anything beyond that, I had to look elsewhere. And so I did, turning to friends and, at times, their siblings and parents for musical guidance.

The first artist I saw in concert was fellow Long Island native Billy Joel at the Nassau Coliseum in Uniondale, New York, when I was fourteen. (I went with a friend and her mother, who seemed oblivious to the plumes of pot smoke emanating from the row ahead of us.) The first album I ever purchased was *Rumours*, by Fleetwood Mac (which I bought only because my friend's older brother was a fan of theirs and I was a fan of his).

During my formative years, disco was king. While I was too young to get past the velvet rope at famed discotheque Studio 54 in Manhattan, I did manage to convince my parents to drop me off at the "teen" nights for the under-18 set at local nightclubs on the north shore of Long Island. Decked out in sateen pants and glittery top, I did my best to mimic the style of the disco dancers I saw on TV. But my natural inclinations were more preppy than disco diva, so I had trouble pulling it off. And while the Bee Gees and Donna Summer were certainly fun to dance to, I found their songs too glossy to *listen* to. Thus I didn't own any of their albums or tune in to disco on the radio.

Instead, thanks to an older neighbor, I discovered the Beatles, who had broken up years before. Their musical experimentation and diversity opened up my ears to a variety of sounds and genres I had never been exposed to. I began stretching beyond the limits of my own environment. And that laid the groundwork for my introduction to country music, and more specifically to Dolly Parton.

It was 1980, and my mother was driving me to the dentist for my annual visit. I was sitting in the front seat, searching on the radio for a song I could sing along to. Near the end of the trip, I heard this angelic voice rising from the car speakers.

It was clear and strong and more pure than anything else on the radio. The song was catchy and the lyrics were clever: "Tumble out of bed and stumble to the kitchen / Pour myself a cup of ambition." Who was this woman singing about her 9-to-5 job? With the urgency only a teenager can feel, I just *had* to know.

We arrived at our destination just as the song was ending. But I wouldn't let my mother turn off the car's ignition until the disc jockey identified the artist (there were no display screens or song identification apps back then). A few moments later, I had the answer. "And that was the new one from Dolly Parton," the DJ said.

Dolly was already a larger-than-life star when I first discovered her. A Grammy and CMA winner beloved by millions, she had a unique voice with a childlike quaver and underlying soul that could deliver heartbreak and joy with equal aplomb. Her delivery wasn't as slick as that of the disco artists who dominated the airwaves at the time. It was genuine—almost sweet—and completely heartfelt. Whatever Dolly sang—whether it was about a 9-to-5 job, a colorful patchwork coat sewed by her mother, or a woman competing for her man—was totally believable.

I was hooked. I couldn't wait to see her in the movie *9 to 5*, for which the song of the same name was written. It was Dolly's feature film debut, but her costars were Hollywood heavyweights: Jane Fonda, Lily Tomlin, and Dabney Coleman. The actors were tasked with balancing the film's humor with its serious message about gender equality. Jane and Lily delivered as expected, but Dolly was a revelation, a natural who more than held her own. In fact, she popped right off the screen. With her blonde wig, southern sass, and innate charm, there was something real and relatable about her. She didn't come across as a music star trying to act; rather, she inhabited the character with the skill and confidence of a screen veteran.

So, I did what I always did when I came across an artist who piqued my interest: I headed to the local record store. There I found a treasure chest of musical gems, and gobbled up *9 to 5 and Odd Jobs, Dolly, Dolly, Dolly*, and *Here You Come Again*. The more I listened to Dolly, the more fascinated I became. I studied her past—from her dirt-poor upbringing with eleven brothers and sisters, to her early performances on local radio in eastern Tennessee.

But what struck me most was the fact that *she wrote the songs that she sang* and she was a *woman*! At the time, few females were double threats (Carole King, Carly Simon, Joni Mitchell). Certainly none looked or sounded like Dolly. Intelligent, bold, and confident, she conquered a male-dominated space and did so without camouflaging or hiding her femininity. She proved you did not have to look or act like a man to be successful. In Dolly's world, lipstick, wigs, and high heels were immaterial to the talent that lies within.

Though short in stature—at a mere five feet tall—Dolly had a towering talent. A pioneer, she created an image and brand long before it was a cottage industry, paving the way for the likes of Madonna, Taylor Swift, and Katy Perry. But even more impressive (though less obvious) was the songwriting. She was prolific even in the 1960s and 1970s, when country's biggest stars relied on hired hands for their biggest hits. She had that unique gift of songcraft—intuitively blending masterful story-telling with unforgettable melodies.

One of my favorites was "Coat of Many Colors," an autobiographical tale about a poor girl whose family was rich with love:

> *My coat of many colors*
> *That my momma made for me*
> *Made only from rags*
> *But I wore it so proudly*
> *Although we had no money*
> *I was rich as I could be*
> *In my coat of many colors*
> *My momma made for me*

Though it had a twang, "Coat of Many Colors" delivered a universal theme of love and acceptance that anyone—even those of us outside of Nashville—could understand. And that's the thing about Dolly's songwriting: it has incredible reach.

Never was that more clear than in 1992. Whitney Houston was the biggest pop star on the planet, and, like Dolly had done a decade earlier, she was making the leap to the big screen in the movie *The Bodyguard*. She also sang the movie's theme song, a soaring love song about the end of a romance called "I Will Always Love You." It was ubiquitous, spending an astounding fourteen weeks atop Billboard's Hot 100 singles charts.

I was in my twenties at this point, at the beginning of my career in entertainment news. I remember getting the press notes on the soundtrack, and I was shocked to see that Dolly was the author of what would become Whitney's biggest hit. How could this have been conceived as a country song when it worked so perfectly as a pop song? Though I had delved into Dolly's catalog as a teenager, I hadn't consumed *all* of it and still had a lot to uncover. And what I found was that Dolly had written the song in 1973, after her professional partnership with the legendary Porter Wagoner had ended.

It was only then that I realized the scope of Dolly Parton's talent. It extended well beyond the hits she's known for. A sure sign of a gifted songwriter is that their work transcends genres, styles, and eras. "I Will Always Love You" is the perfect example of that.

One of the benefits of being an entertainment news journalist is that I get to meet my idols. I have been lucky enough to have interviewed Dolly several times over the years. The first time came about ten years into my career, on the set of her TV movie *Unlikely Angel*. I was so nervous—I can't remember what I asked her or how she responded. All I recall is that we retreated to her trailer and she was as warm and friendly as I had hoped.

My most memorable interactions with her came years later, after my anxiety melted away and I was far less starstruck. Around 2014, when I was working as a producer for *Access Hollywood,* we had a special segment in which we asked songwriters about the stories behind their classic hits. For sentimental reasons, I chose "9 to 5" for Dolly.

We did the interview in a dressing room right after her appearance on *The Today Show* in New York, and there was activity all around us—until Dolly started revealing how she came up with the song idea. She started tapping her long acrylic nails together as if they were instruments, and said that's what she was doing during a break one day on the set of the movie *9 to 5*. The room grew quiet as Dolly explained that the sound reminded her of a typewriter—the writing instrument favored by secretaries before the proliferation of computers—and that inspired her to write the song.

I was struck by two things that day: first—Dolly kept perfect rhythm with her fingernails. And second—how amazing it was that she could turn something so mundane into a pop and country classic.

My most meaningful conversation with Dolly came after an interview in New York in 2008, not too long after my mother passed away. She and Dolly had the same birthday (though a few years apart). And I mentioned it to Dolly. I told her how special my mom was and that I had recently lost her to cancer. And I will never forget how Dolly responded. She looked at me with compassion and asked if she reminded me of my mother.

Although my mom was blonde and petite like Dolly, she wasn't southern or bold or done up (she favored the minimal makeup look). And yet, when Dolly asked that question, I found myself saying yes. Because, like Dolly, my mom was strong yet feminine, and candid yet never mean. And she was enveloped by this ray of light that was bright and sunny no matter how nasty the forecast. (Not even cancer could dim it.) Dolly has that, too.

So I told Dolly that, yes, she did remind me of my mom. With a lump in my throat the size of an apple, I wasn't able to say much more. Dolly grabbed my hand and told me she was honored—honored!—to be compared to my mom.

In reality, I wouldn't be the woman I am today without Dolly or my mom and the examples they both set. I wouldn't be as independent or successful. And I certainly wouldn't be as happy. And while I do believe that Dolly was truly touched that I would compare her to someone I deeply loved, it is I who was privileged to have even been in the presence of such true greatness.

EMMYLOU HARRIS

Common Ground
in an Uncommon Love

ALI BERLOW

The news of his death was incomparable news. Whether the plane crashed or didn't. Whether he was on it or wasn't. Or when he died, or where. The goneness was the same. The summation of dead is dead. Details meant next to nothing here. Dennis, my Dennis, was gone.

I stumbled out of my kitchen, through the screen door to the back porch. Perhaps I had been cooking dinner. Probably was. The monotones of summer green were smothering. There was no sound I could hear except the wail. Someone was wailing. It was me, though I didn't recognize the voice. The sound came from the center of the earth, a geologic rupture. After one breath. And then another. Being left alone in the world so abruptly, out at sea without Dennis, my compass. My husband Sam knew better than to come close. As if he was watching a wild animal writhing in pain, he stayed at bay, a good distance away. And let me rage against the universe until I gave up, and the universe continued on.

A portion of his obituary read: "Dr. Dennis Arthur 'Kilonzo' Doughty, a US State Department Warden in Zanzibar, died on August 23, 2005, en route to his home in Stone Town, Zanzibar. He was 62."

How do I possibly explain? The chosen family. This one person who crossed into my life by chance—destiny, I suppose. He was at once like my lover, brother, father, companion, keeper, storyteller, deepest friend. Dennis was the person who set me free and, most importantly, saved my life by sending me away. Dennis was the one who told me to go home. My time in Kenya had to come to an end at the young age of twenty-two or twenty-three. It was my time to leave and go back to the United States. And because I trusted Dennis with my life, I listened to him and did as he said.

———

A body's senses seem to vanish in grief. A cascade of shockwaves in a vortex of loss. Grief blinds. Dumbs. Taste dulls. Touch is distant: needed, yet too intimate. But sounds—they are the armature to life. They are what we navigate by. Coffee grinding, the dog's claws clicking on the floor. Bacon fat sizzling in a hot iron skillet, a stock pot simmering.

It was Emmylou's *Red Dirt Girl* in which I could finally hear grief, whether I wanted to or not. Part hymnal, the album's prayers and songs about solitude and losing love helped bring me back to my senses, returned me to awake.

"The Pearl," the opening track of *Red Dirt Girl*, played on WMVY, our local independent radio station. Emmy counting off "One, two, three . . ." was something I could mimic like a child—it was as if she took my hand and said "trust me." I did, and I held on tight, counting with her to the downbeat. I followed along out of my daze and back to my earthly plain. Emmylou's music wrapped around my loss, making grief no less intolerable but reminding me of the fragility of life, what it means to love, and especially the truth of never having to give away, or get over, that love, ever.

I found that in motherhood, beyond words, my sense of hearing became finely attuned to the nuances and language of my babies' swallows, laughter, and cries. Raising my boys opened my body to sound, just as it was changed by the stretch marks from birthing and nursing. Yet when Dennis died, in that voicelessness of grief, even the sounds of home, routine, and responsibilities fell on now-deafened ears.

That was when Emmylou's songs summoned me, intersecting with my life and grounding me when there were no words, no sounds. Emmylou sang, unexpectedly, to the searing cuts of an uncommon love lost. Of grief. Of the equally searing embrace of always loving, no matter what, because there is no other choice but to do so.

She was a voice, a gleaming presence in the darkness. I didn't know about her own muse and mentor, Gram Parsons, who was lost at twenty-six to an overdose in Joshua Tree, California. Exotic and knowing, he took a young single mother/folk singer and opened the door for her to the hard country music of George Jones, the Louvin Brothers' close-harmony heartbreak bluegrass, the trucker boogie of "Six Days on the Road." The Rolling Stones even wrote "Wild Horses" for him (or about him).

They dueted, and toured together. She'd sung on his record that was about to come out. He was a gorgeous wild child who rescued her, the dark-haired Modigliani-looking girl singing in a Georgetown bar, and transformed her life. Lifted her from obscurity, showed her the ropes, the Nudie suits and the rock & roll life. Then—POOF!—he was gone.

She was left alone with a legacy at odds with modern country and too traditional for California country rock. But more than that, her north star, her peer, was gone; her spark was extinguished.

But let me tell you more about Dennis. Because these details are important. Though he had little in common with Parsons, beyond the dashing reckless spirit and visionary habitation of this world that they shared, he was bound to me in much the same way that Emmylou carries Parsons with her.

Dennis told the best stories. He was dashingly handsome, with sparkling blue, mischievous eyes. Full mustache, always impeccably dressed. He was twenty years my senior, from Wisconsin. He had built a respectable veterinary practice in Connecticut. Dennis was also gay. He moved to Kenya in the mid-eighties, and that's when and where our paths crossed. It was in the wake of the deadly AIDS epidemic that ravaged his life and his chosen family, which was on the verge of becoming a community before the HIV virus decimated it.

He'd later joke that he'd let his membership in the Moral Majority run out long ago—but he kept them close, to know what they were up to. Having lost so many friends to AIDS, and also suffering due to the ignorance, stigma, and prejudice around the disease, he left, moved to another continent—truly another world, a far more exotic one. And that's where I, also Wisconsin-born and -raised, found him.

When Dennis died, we had just reconnected over that last year. I was forty, grown, yet on that visit, what would turn out to be his last to the States, I found myself once again dazzled.

He stayed with me and my family, taking a break from doctor appointments and seeing old friends, those who were still around. When we were younger and together in Africa, we lived moment to moment, respectful of, yet unencumbered by, the past. But sitting on my porch, reminiscing, I prodded him some, asking about his choice to leave. We drank gin and tonics. He smoked cigarettes with style, while I coughed my way through one or two. The gay community that he knew, that he came from, had dried up. He told me it was "gone, wiped out"; he knew that if he did return to the States, he'd probably just be looked at as a weird old faggot. Though he said it with wry wit, I could see it broke his heart.

As for me, my life had filled up with marriage, two kids, a house, my home. There were cats and an old black lab. When I heard Emmylou playing on the radio in my kitchen, I had no context for it, and no idea who she was. But that silvery, featherweight tone seemed like a tether between the ethereal and the earthbound. She was singing about never getting over loving and losing someone. She, without ever intending to, granted me permission to feel those things, to mourn for and lament those I loved. Even, or perhaps especially, those people in my life who were undefined by basic categories.

In "Bang the Drum Slowly," I heard the simple, and so human, too-late regrets. About the questions I never asked Dennis before he died. The answers I never got to hear. How time with our loved ones is so fleeting, how much we take for granted.

I heard Emmylou sing about the things I had taken for granted or, worse, lacked the awareness of to ask. I also heard her sing to a patriot and a war hero, her own father. I think of Dennis that way—he was a hero for surviving AIDS and the politics and judgment inflicted upon people who had it. Though he had lived for over twenty years in Africa before he died, he never waivered in who he was: Dennis, my Dennis, was an American. He had to leave the States in order to live his life. He saved himself by moving abroad, to live in a freedom and an acceptance he didn't have here, but he never forgot his home. Or, as his visit showed me, the people he loved so fiercely and without conditions.

———

Growing up in Wisconsin, I figured I was Mary in Bruce Springsteen's "Thunder Road." I was that girl with my dress waving, sitting next to the boy who was driving away, to anywhere but there. In high school, my soundtrack was *Greetings from Asbury Park, N.J.* and *The Wild, the Innocent & the E Street Shuffle.* Springsteen was the road, the escape, and his songs fanned my yearning to leave town as fast as I could.

But after a failed first semester at the University of Colorado in Boulder, where there were too many drugs and too much money, I came back to Madison, where I knew the sidewalks and streets so well I could find my way home in my sleep. Knowing now how much I underappreciated home and my sense of place, I responded the only way I could: by going to Africa.

And in Africa, I met Dennis. In Nairobi, on its backstreets, under the magenta bougainvillea. We wandered the dirt roads and markets and the beaches of Malindi, off the coast of Kenya. We were in the same intensive Swahili language–immersion course: strangers in a strange land, looking for belonging and adventure.

It was Dennis who welcomed me, ran with me, drank with me, grounded me as I went into that wild world. Ultimately, it was Dennis, recognizing I was living beyond my physical limits, who sent me home.

In those African travels I had found what I'd been seeking in the songs of Springsteen: I ran faster, traveled deeper, sought harder, and feared not the night. I drew new constellations of my own desire. I had tasted, populated those songs that I'd grown up pining over.

But when Dennis died, I was in my early forties and deep into the life of mothering. It was Emmylou who found and settled my troubled soul. She led me, with her songs, through grief in all its honor, glory, and ragged edges.

She was a mother, too: often singing about being still, seeking that place of reflection. I felt seen. No longer was I a girl chasing dreams on a highway out of town. I was a mom, responsible for my babies; the highway was for another time. With Emmy and *Red Dirt Girl*, I could be still. I could understand the arc of my life through experience, through clear waters instead of the angst-muddied rivers of rebellion and youth.

I was always an outsider in my mothering peer group. How could I possibly explain Dennis, or what losing him meant to me, over juice boxes on playdates? What if someone said casually, "You'll get over it"? Well-intentioned, but utterly missing the truth, the blinding ache and chaos in my heart. So I shut myself away.

What I heard in Emmylou's songs offered common ground in an uncommon love, the absolute truth of loving Dennis and being loved back. The trajectory of my entire life as lived, not through a prism of what I think it should have been or yet could be. Right there, in that moment: the beauty and, yes, this jagged arrowhead cutting into me, making it hard to breathe, harder still to sleep.

In Emmylou, I also saw a woman who had long brown hair, as I had. And unbraced teeth, as I do. The white-on-white cover of *Stumble into Grace* became my coda to *Red Dirt Girl*. That cover showed me truths about life beyond even the music: it was so angelic, spiritual, yet somehow real. Looking at her, I saw me.

Emmylou and me, we own that hair, silver now. We own the right to be beautiful as we age. We are lucky. "Lost Unto This World" and "Can You Hear Me Now" accompanied me into the next roads I took. Musically and otherwise.

Timing is everything, of course. When and where a song falls on your ears. What gets to you when you need the song or the artist most. Emmylou was the guiding voice in my (re)education, providing a new sense of gravity in a world without Dennis. I followed her lyrically the best that I could, and I let the music take me when necessary.

Many years of my life have been spent being busy. Busy with homemaking. Raising children. "What is worth doing?" were the words I would ask myself in the busiest of years as a young mother; they still resonate today. Of course, raising a child is worth doing. But finding your voice is also worth doing, whatever odd paths you may follow to get there.

Emmylou's path is a testament to this, with her sundry collaborations, from Mark Knopfler to Neil Young and from Rodney Crowell to Linda Ronstadt and Dolly Parton, and with the trips she has taken into bluegrass, gospel, concept albums, atmospherics, and meditations on the truly adult life.

I was a novice food writer when my kids were still home. I took my time in becoming a writer and calling myself one, because I am formally untrained. Fake-it-till-you-make-it was how I approached my craft, and my writing grew from my life. But that's kind of like being a mom, too. My break came when the local NPR station began airing a series of my essays about cooking, food, and sharing sustenance, "A Cook's Notebook." Through those weekly deadlines and that steep learning curve, I found my voice.

It is by doing that we learn, by honing that we become proficient, by trusting that we get there. I know that there is no substitute for the layers of days and words that went into my pursuit of writing, of food, of family.

Sometimes I hear twenty-somethings say out loud how fifty-somethings careers' are over. I will say this now: it is a privilege and a blessing to live to this age, to find your voice through how you live and experience the world. That wisdom, those textures, can't be taught.

Four decades into her musical career, Emmylou Harris stands for her art and for a life lived authentically; she honors her gifts of artistry and humanity. There are awards and charity work, music to make and friends to love. When I look at Emmylou, who worked as a waitress, then became a young single mother who moved back to her parents' house to raise her first daughter, I see a woman who never stopped singing. She played lounges and fern bars just so she could sing while working a day job, because the music was that strong inside her.

It's startling, when I listen to Emmylou's early records: the youngness of her voice, how almost tentative she sounds, even surprising herself. I sense that she is thinking: "How could 'that' come from me?" Her earlier self comes through in her music's searching and simplicity. The songs she sings today have an emotional complexity that her earlier records, as good as they are, just don't. And that makes total sense, because all that life had yet to happen, all that insight had yet to come.

There's no artistry in trying to hold onto youth. Just as innocence is precious in its moment, so are all the phases of a woman's life. Those stretch marks . . . they are worthy and full of truth, story, and praise.

I see in Emmylou a woman who is graceful yet fierce, never giving up or compromising her art. Like a drop of water in a wave, she is the circular integration of experience and energy, moving ever so slightly forward in every single orbit, every pass, incorporating more and moving closer and closer to shore, to cresting completely in emotion, connection, story, song, and harmony.

Though it's hard to comprehend how one drop of water can make a difference, it's harder to believe one person's actions can also make a difference, in the face of the odds against us. But taking those first steps, no matter how far off success may be—like Emmy persevering in mothering her two daughters while breaking musical ground across genres and times—is how you have to begin.

It's through food that I turned feeling isolated in my own kitchen into connecting and reaching out to my community. It was in writing about food and engaging with farmers, fishermen, food chain workers, policy makers, and activists—though I had no "pedigree," and nothing in my resume suggested that I was qualified to work for a more just, equitable, and resilient food community—that I learned the things I needed to know. I knew then, as I do now, that seeking to expand awareness, and support food systems at their source, was something very much worth doing.

Now I challenge myself not to be the writer or activist, mother or wife or friend I was yesterday, one year, or ten years ago, but to merely be in the moment, open to what that brings—and who I need to be in that space. I wasn't looking for Emmylou. I didn't expect her and I didn't think—or know how badly—I needed her songs.

It's not that *my* Emmylou is better than someone else's Emmylou, maybe her romping honky-tonk incarnation or that *Blue Kentucky Girl* who covered Paul Simon's "The Boxer." My version of Emmylou doesn't diminish the country rock of her mid-career, or the Americana canon she defined. Each of those versions speaks deep to the person who embraces it; as with the activism I do, it is people recognizing what they need in her and responding in kind.

When Dennis was gone, and the finality of that hit me, there was nothing else—save the tsunami wave of grief that didn't quite topple me. Frozen in pain, anguished beyond language, I found Emmylou Harris: a silvery voice on a cloud of acoustic instruments speaking straight to my soul. It wasn't about country music, or folk, or Americana, or even just sheer beauty; it was my pulse and my breath.

⟋ℓℓ⟋

BARBARA MANDRELL

Lubbock in the Rearview Mirror

SHELBY MORRISON

There is a well-debated theory that so many great musicians come out of West Texas because of the arrival of aliens. In August and September of 1951, formations of alien lights, forever mythologized as the "Lubbock Lights," were seen over the Great Plains. The lights were one of the first great UFO cases in the United States and were highly publicized. Did the alien energy that was beamed to the ground infect talented babies with great musical potential? Another theory is that the mosquito repellent misted into the wind by the DDT trucks that went up and down the roads was inhaled by the young and gifted. Or perhaps it was energy from the Ogallala Aquifer, a massive underground reservoir that lives under the Caprock, giving life to the endless miles of cotton and sorghum fields. Or maybe it was simply the isolation of Lubbock, which is about five hours from anywhere.

Personally, I believe that the magic of the music is in the wind—literally in the wind. I remember picking small bits of red dirt out of my teeth in high school, as our gym coaches didn't think a Dust-Bowl-era-type haboob was reason enough to cancel track practice. The wind was endless, tossing up layers of soil from at least sixty miles in every direction and flinging the particles everywhere. Dusting your house at least three times a day was normal, and forget about ever wearing lip gloss. Along with the dust, the wind also carried that magic music across the flat land, and you could hear it everywhere you went. Also, the creatively inclined had to either make music or sit around listening to it, because there is nothing else to do except go to church.

Before I truly understood what the Good Book meant about choosing the righteous path versus what the forbidden lyrics of songs were coaxing me to do, I understood Johnny Paycheck, Bob Wills, Buddy Holly, Johnny Cash, and Willie, Waylon, and the boys. The music always-on-the-wind created a craving in me, and it didn't even matter that none of the artists were like me, a girl. Then, one night, sitting in front of the old box color TV, I watched the *Barbara Mandrell and the Mandrell Sisters* television show for the first time, and was introduced to Barbara, Irlene, and Louise.

Barbara was the oldest; I was also the oldest in my family, with two younger sisters. She was—to my six-year-old mind— "a girl, like me" *and* a "big girl, like my mom." And she was a vision! Damn, she had her own TV show and she could sing *and* play all the instruments.

I yearned for the confidence, fearlessness, glamour, strength, and kindness that the Mandrells radiated. I wanted to be a part of their sisterhood. Barbara Mandrell helped to shape who I am: a confident woman, a woman who believes in herself. Barbara was in charge, she had a purpose, and she inspired me to tuck my tiny Wranglers into my red Roper cowboy boots, cinch my belt buckle, crack my knuckles, and get to work to find *my* purpose. She was everything I wanted to be.

Lubbock, Texas, has more churches per capita then any other city in America. It was simple, really: you could do whatever you liked on a Saturday night (no holds barred), as long as you didn't mess with another person's family, tractor, or property. And as long as your tail was in that church pew Sunday morning, all was forgiven. As a young girl growing up in such a black-and-white world (or a reddish-brown world, if you took a look around at all the dirt), how could I get it wrong? The rule was that no female should have an opinion of her own about anything, and if she did, she could not say it out loud. Even now, in the Baptist churches of West Texas, women are not allowed to stand up and pray out loud in front of the congregation. I believe that my mother took my sisters and me to almost every church in the Lubbock area, and then promptly dragged us out because of that fact.

I came to realize, from the stretched-out necklines of my Sunday dresses and from my discovery of Barbara Mandrell, that being bound to the Lubbock path just wasn't for me. I wanted to scream my thoughts out loud to anyone who would listen—if only anyone would. As I watched Barbara and her sisters every week, and saw her joyfully picking the instruments, I also picked up on the fact that Barbara wanted a lot more. I wanted a lot more, too—the stakes were high.

What would happen if I broke ranks and went rogue and got out of Lubbock, shook off the red dust and flew? Would my church, my God, accept me? Would my family? As it turned out, I never cared too much about the opinions of my fellow West Texans, and anyhow, I was too weird to understand them.

Barbara Mandrell was born with instincts that we, as a society, typically describe as masculine: an astute business sense, a willingness to speak her mind, a stubbornness that her way was the right way. Because Barbara was gifted with talent and had the natural confidence it took to follow her dreams, the fact that she was a girl didn't mean that she couldn't do or be anything she wanted to do or be in her life, with her family and God beside her.

The Mandrell show always started with an announcement, "Ladies and gentlemen, Barbara Mandrell!," followed by the energetic, yet graceful, entrance of Barbara onto the stage, where she proclaimed, "My sisters, Irlene and Louise!" All three of the ladies were beautiful, both in the traditional sense and because of the bond of sisterhood they very clearly shared. And, oh, the dresses! For each episode, the sisters wore dresses that were individual to each of them, but matched somehow.

Covered in shiny fabric, beads, sequins, and sparkles, they were colorful, glamorous, and always made them look like they were floating across the stage.

In one of my favorite episodes, in the opening monologue between Barbara and her sisters, Louise and Irlene came onstage wearing dresses that were a bit more revealing than Barbara's. As the oldest, Barbara's duty was to make sure that her sisters knew that their dresses were not appropriate, and they, in turn, called her stuffy and old-fashioned. To this, Barbara responded by pulling the sleeves off of her dress to reveal an outfit just as sexy and flashy as those of her younger sisters, and they all proceeded to perform a wiggly song-and-dance number. As sassy, fierce, and magnetic as they were, they were also wholesome, embodying confidence, strength, femininity, and independence.

With two younger sisters of my own, I innately knew the importance of "setting a good example." It didn't take long to convince my little followers to join in the fun, and we would all pretend to be the Mandrells, arguing over which of mom's old twirler costumes we were going to put on, learning the lessons together, as sisters.

Louise was "the Beautiful One," Irlene was "the Funny and Naïve One," and Barbara was the leader, or "the Bossy One." These were the roles assigned to the sisters to play on television. They are much more complicated women than these stereotypes, but these roles showed a balance among the relationships of sisters, of women. Being an eldest sister, I already understood the delicate, intense, and loving bond that exists between sisters. However, what I learned from the Mandrells was that sisterhood extends from your blood sisters to the sisterhood among all women. Whether you are related or not, the bonds between women in friendship and in the business world rely on support.

I have had many female bosses and colleagues who were not afraid to help me rise above—to get that promotion, to challenge myself with projects I wasn't sure I could handle, to ask for a bigger raise. In friendship too, we women support each other through love, loss, and all of life. To give support; to treat each other with kindness, patience, and humor; to celebrate each other in our accomplishments instead of being envious—I learned these things from the Mandrells, as did the 40 million other people who tuned in each week to watch them on television.

By the time I graduated from college at Texas Tech, in Lubbock, I had become an expert on where I was from. I had mastered the art of the "alien" language of Lubbock and was a mini-celebrity in my own right. To pay for college, I had bartended at the best and biggest honky-tonk at the time, the Midnight Rodeo. The uniform was black spandex pants with suspenders, but I cut my hair super short and drew fake tattoos on my arms with black sharpie markers so the cowboys wouldn't get the wrong idea. The drinks were good and cheap, they had live music once in a while, and all of the cowboys and frat boys paid my tuition.

The Rodeo was best known for its racetrack-style dance floor that circled a center bar. The bar was transformed on live-music nights, and I got to see the likes of Chris LeDoux, Mark Chesnutt, and an early version of the Dixie Chicks just as wild-child vocalist Natalie Maines joined the band. My duties eventually expanded, and I was allowed to help handle the artists.

Getting ready for work, pulling on my spandex and putting on my black lipstick, I would grab my hairbrush and belt out Barbara's "sleeping single in a double bed . . ." As I worked, I would chat up the "music" people I knew about Barbara. "Hey, did you know that the Mandrells closed every show with a gospel song?" Her voice was never far from my mind, pushing me to get the hell out of that dust trap.

I plotted and planned my escape routes with the words from a Mac Davis song, "Happiness is Lubbock, Texas, in your rearview mirror," in my mind. My early attempts, though wholehearted, were full of fear and self-doubt. I just didn't know how to get out. I asked myself, what would Barbara do? I had to keep in motion.

Ironically, there were many roads into Lubbock; it was known as the Hub City because, back when the cotton industry was born, all four of the big highways *and* the Sante Fe Railroad converged in Lubbock. Those roads led *out* too, didn't they?

Postcollege, I should've become a teacher or a secretary, or gotten married and started a West Texas clan of my own. That was expected, it was even easy. I just couldn't . . . I wouldn't. Instead, I became a waitress, which was acceptable. But eventually my mother reached her limit with me and started digging through the want ads. And there it was, in black and white, a part-time gig at the new music museum (and only music museum in a 500-mile radius): the job of gallery assistant at the Buddy Holly Center—a shining jewel (with horn-rimmed glasses) in the dry, bleak landscape. That was my start.

I, for lack of a better term, was "discovered" in 2003 when the Rock & Roll Hall of Fame hosted a tribute event for Buddy Holly. I flew up to Cleveland to attend the event, and I'm not sure whether it was because I knew every Holly-related person there, or because my brain was filled with music knowledge that I was happy to share with anyone, or because of my West Texas charm, or all of those things—but, months later, I was offered a job at the Hall of Fame if I was willing to pack up my life and move to Ohio.

In fact, the president of the Hall of Fame at the time, Terry Stewart, flew down to Lubbock and told my mother that he was going to offer me a job, and the only reason I wouldn't take it would be if she told me not to. (Then he asked if Lubbock had a Church's Chicken restaurant.) How country is that? My new boss asking my mom if she would give her permission. Holy prayers, I was moving out of Lubbock—I was on my way!

———

By the time Louise and Irlene came into the Mandrell family, Barbara was already on the road to becoming a professional musician. Her mother taught her how to play the accordion and the bass and how to read music. Barbara was born with the

musical knack; she could play music the way others are naturally good at sports or math. Barbara was five and a half when
Louise was born, and then Irlene came along eighteen months
later. As the Mandrell Family Band, they traveled and performed
together until Barbara was married to naval officer Ken Dud-
ney in 1967, when she was eighteen years old. But a year later
she heard the siren call of country music again, and the family
band resumed.

Louise and Irlene believed in their sister and had no prob-
lem rejoining the family group. They showed true sisterhood
in supporting their older sister and realizing all of their dreams
together. Even when Louise and Irlene had aspirations of their
own, professionally and personally, they always supported each
other. All three of them were proficient at singing and playing
instruments, and their versatility is still impressive today. But
what drew people to them, to their music and their personali-
ties, went deeper than a pretty face, a lovely dress, or even a good
song; it was that they really were what they purported to be—a
family band.

Since leaving Lubbock in the rearview mirror, and now living
in northeast Ohio and relishing the lake-effect snows and good
people of Cleveland, I have found a new appreciation for where
I was raised. In the rock & roll world, Buddy Holly is royalty, and
because I share my roots with him, it gives me a certain mys-
tique. And Lubbock itself has become endearing, with its empty,
flat spaces, its two-tone horizon of sky and dirt, and its serious
lack of colorful flora and fauna. We call it "Lubbock Ugly," but
we can see the beauty where others do not. And I am incredibly
lucky to have a supportive family there, just like Barbara and her
sisters had.

Barbara Mandrell won many awards in her career; she was
the only female artist to win the coveted Country Music Association's Entertainer of the Year prize twice, in 1980 and 1981,
until Taylor Swift equaled her in 2009 and 2011. But regardless
of what awards she has won or which of her songs have topped
the charts, the lasting legacy of Barbara Mandrell, for me, will be

her positive spirit and the choices she has made to live a life full of confidence, strength, sisterhood, fearlessness, and faith.

I just celebrated twenty years in the music industry with a promotion—and a brand new office. It was a significant milestone. Recently, I found myself sitting in a café eating a piece of cake to celebrate my promotion, and I started thinking back on the bumpy, dusty, twisty road I took to get there. As I ate that piece of cake, I got choked up thinking of how far I had come. It wasn't the "peanuts in my coke" that Barbara sang of in "I Was Country (When Country Wasn't Cool)," but "tears on my cake" could just as easily be the lyrics to a country song.

I started out as nothing more than a speck of dust from Lubbock, Texas, and now I have my dream job as Director of Artist and VIP Relations at the Rock & Roll Hall of Fame. The lessons I learned from Barbara Mandrell about being fearless, strong, and confident, and especially about being supportive of my sisters in this industry, have been paramount to my success. And they were only the first of many lessons that strong female artists have taught me.

Cyndi Lauper taught me to always be true to myself. If it wasn't right for someone else, it didn't mean it wasn't right for me. Wanda Jackson taught me that you can be sexy on your own terms. I have followed Patti Smith around a venue as her handler, picking up items she left behind—glasses, notebook, salad fork—which I would then gladly return to her to hear her laugh at my jokes; from her I learned about the magic of deep intelligence. I have received fashion lessons from Debbie Harry, and I learned the importance of accepting your own darkness from Rosanne Cash.

There was more: I picked up fierce, gritty street knowledge from Martha Reeves; glamour, poise, and how to be a dignitary from Mary Wilson; sweet silliness from Lisa Loeb; truth from Melissa Etheridge; more about the blessings of family from Sheryl Crow; self-acceptance and never giving up on yourself from Kesha; the importance of never losing your inspiration from Ariana Grande; and the value of kindness to all from Elle King.

My Aunt Fairy once told me, not long before I moved up north, that I had a great uncle who was a fiddle player in Bob Wills's band. The family plot, on my dad's side, is located in Quitaque, Texas, northeast of Lubbock and near Turkey, Texas, Wills's home base. With that news, I immediately felt the bond between music and family rushing back to me, like the feeling of the shag carpet under my feet as I danced to the Mandrells in my living room. Perhaps I was abducted by those aliens, spinning in the Lubbock Lights, and this has all been a dream. But then I can picture myself singing Barbara's "Crackers" at a karaoke bar, picking the dust out of my drink, and I know that it is real.

~ele~

TANYA TUCKER

———

Punk Country and Sex Wide Open

HOLLY GLEASON

Cleveland, Ohio, is the Rock & Roll Capital of the World. Self-annointed, perhaps, but winning enough *Rolling Stone* Readers' Polls for Favorite Radio Station and raising the funds to land the Rock & Roll Hall of Fame, it cashes the check as the city where rock & roll is exalted above all. Why Cleveland? The weather—especially in winter, fall, and spring—is rugged, and, at least back in the day, the sports teams were perpetual losers and the toxic fallout from the local industries saw the Cuyahoga River catch fire and Lake Erie's chemical buildup kill all its fish.

But the landscape of factories belching black clouds of smelter smoke, oozing muddy rainbow swirls of shimmering chemical runoff, and buildings with busted, boarded-up windows made for a toughness that gave rock & roll's furor a fertile place to take root. Bruce Springsteen, Todd Rundgren, Mott the Hoople, Meatloaf, and U2 were just a few who caught fire in my hometown long before the rest of the nation caught up—and knowing those acts before the rest of your peers did gave a kid serious social standing.

Blessed by the turquoise glow of an 8-track player that had FM capabilities, I was baptized nightly by WMMS, the album-oriented FM station that won all those *Rolling Stone* Polls. Aerosmith, Dr. Hook, Artful Dodger, local favorites the Michael Stanley Band and talking blues folk raver Alex Bevan, Little Feat, King Crimson, the Kinks, Lynyrd Skynyrd, Bonnie Raitt, and the holy trinity of Brit Rock—the Beatles, the Stones, and the Who—all swept into my bedroom long after I was supposed to be asleep. Igniting my imagination, they reinforced a shy girl with the knowledge every kid my age craved.

With my Shetland wool Fair Isle sweater, straight-legged corduroys, button-down Oxford shirt, and sleek brown hair side-parted, I was an American ideal. A championship golfer, at least locally, I hung in pro shop backrooms, learning the canon of Genesis's *Nursery Crimes* and *Trick of the Tail* with the same acuity I applied in school to understanding long division, mitosis, and Mesopotamia.

Country music was for hicks and hayseed golf pros. Not something to bother with, let alone give serious attention to. Sure, we'd watched *The Johnny Cash Show* every week, to see the black-clad man himself bring a mélange of roots music and subtle social commentary into our conservative home; and my father owned Jimmy Dean's "Big Bad John," in part because his own name was John. But beyond that? We were educated people, and refined.

Country music? No, thank you.

Then the *Cleveland Scene* review hit, written in some kind of Jethro Bodine trucker patois, as much leering peep-show lechery as serious music criticism. But I saw the words "Angel from Montgomery" on one of those late nights under the covers of my white-linen canopy bed, and I was intrigued.

Tanya Tucker, not much older than me, had gone rock & roll. Or so the review seemed to be saying, beyond the commentary on her form in a skintight pair of leather pants that seemed to have more lascivious punch than Jim Morrison and Elvis combined. But, "how rock & roll could some hillbilly be?" went my fourteen-year-old mind; this was followed by, "But 'Angel from Montgomery' is some kind of rural soul . . ."

And then I put it out of my mind.

Tanya Tucker had confronted me a year or two earlier in a one-column ad in *Seventeen* magazine, her hair a thick cloud of Farrah Fawcett curls on the cover of an album called *Lizzie & the Rainman*. The ad made an impression because it said she was fifteen or sixteen, and it boasted about all the number-one singles she'd had.

"Yeah, whatever," I thought. I wasn't big on the Partridge Family or the Osmonds, either. To me, the records made by young white kids were confections, ear candy that would rot your brain with too much sugar and not enough substance. The ad briefly registered, and that was all. Beyond that, well, there were golf tournaments to screw up and my ongoing battles with dyslexia and higher learning to focus on.

Tanya Tucker wasn't worth the mental space.

By the time that *Scene* review hit, I was in full thrall to another, even younger, girl: Rachel Sweet. Signed to STIFF—the punk label whose roster included Ian ("Sex & Drugs & Rock & Roll," "Hit Me With Your Rhythm Stick") Drury, Lene ("Lucky Number") Lovich, the glorious Elvis Costello, and configurations involving Nick Lowe and Dave Edmunds—Sweet was being marketed as a jailbait truth-teller with a voice like a buzz saw and a throwback sensibility that echoed Ronnie Spector with a little bit of backroom holler queen.

Hailing from Akron—just a short drive away—she could almost be me! On the back of an album cover that saw her in blue jeans and a rugby shirt, lollipop in her mouth, or on the front cover in a—most likely some boy's—leather jacket and a striped T-shirt, she was a doppelgänger for every girl throbbing to be something more, something wild, something brazen, something . . . gone.

When she blared raw strychnine and sex, "Sitting around in the Firestone parking lot / And it's alright / Talking 'bout boys, and who's taking what / And bands we could see tonight . . . ," that was a truth we were all living right there in northern Ohio. The ska rhythms, the tangled neon guitar, it felt subversive.

Equally subversive was the juke rock/teen angst shuffle "Pin a Medal on Mary," a vitriol hiss bomb about losing your boy to a tart with far looser morality, or the stop-start, tropically humid "It's So Different Here," cooed in a sweet little-girl soprano of disorientation and hope.

That subversion obscured a truth about Sweet's *Fool Around* debut. The cello-basted "Wildwood Saloon" was a straight country lament of a strung-out working girl with a broken-hearted caution, and Elvis Costello's stately "Angel from Montgomery"–esque "Stranger in the House" was delivered with vintage George Jones sorrow-gulping stoicism.

Sweet was punk, through 'n' through. She was featured on the Be Stiff! Tour—with Lovich, Drury, Wreckless Eric—and was opening for Southside Johnny. No Hill William, she! With a big-girl voice and a preternatural sexuality that flickered with a certain toughness, you could tell she *knew* things . . . and that knowing transcended.

Cocooned in that smugness, I walked into Record Theater at the Golden Gate Shopping Center on a slushy spring Saturday, ten dollars in my pocket—and a will to bring home some new gateway drug. That's when I saw the stand-up.

A lifesize cutout of a hot-rod redhead in a skin-clutching red spandex catsuit, dropped low in the back, her back to the camera and head tossed high in half challenge, half come-on. I stopped in my tracks, blinked three times, and had . . . *nothing*. There was a mic up and poised just beyond Tanya's lips, cord wrapped through her fingers, then falling down, around and between her legs.

My mouth went dry, the room lost air. In her other hand, the one slung low behind a curved haunch that Beyoncé would die for, was a lashed-together pack of dynamite sticks. The implication— obvious to a girl virtually raised by golf pros who were constantly on the late-night prowl for poontang—was literal and suggested, metaphoric and packaged. This one, boys, is ready to blow.

So overt, so full-tilt, so frankly unapologetic, it slammed into me in a way that left me stunned. *What the . . . ?!* I went to look at

Aerosmith records, to debate whether or not *this* was the week I bought *Dream On* ... then considered whether I really wanted to rappel backwards into Springsteen via *The Wild, The Innocent & The E Street Shuffle*. And there was the matter of Carole King's *Rhyme & Reason*.

But every aisle I went down, every corner I turned, there was Tucker in her hot tomato plastic lip gloss, seriously pitched stilt-heel slides, and a look of defiant "Try Me" on her face. She wasn't picking a fight, but what was it? *What* WAS *it*?

Reluctantly, I swerved back to the featured albums endcap— and lifted *TNT* from the rack. It was really bad set design: rough-hewn faux wood nailed together to suggest a construction site, the album title stenciled on a plank. Those black leather pants worn tight enough to cut off circulation, and that mic chord again snaking between her thighs.

As a two-dimensional take on the dynamite business, it was way too *Hee Haw*. Related to the Austin Powder Company by marriage—my uncle had wed one of the owner's daughters—I saw the hard work those men did and the dignity they had. And yet, having seen enough *Playboy* centerfolds on the backs of grown men's doors, I had a feeling they wouldn't be offended.

Furrowing my brow, I flipped the record over and began poring over the credits. A Buddy Holly song ("Not Fade Away"), a Chuck Berry song ("Brown Eyed Handsome Man"), and an Elvis song ("Heartbreak Hotel") suggested a woman breaking away from what she was—and leaning into the name-brand fundamentals.

Coming into her own, she needed to make her own kind of music. Already established as a franchise—some kind of kid torch singer for the melodramatic inbred set—she was making her way slowly. The fact that she'd recorded a Phil Everly song that wasn't an Everly Brothers' classic, and that she'd been brave enough to take a pass at Bonnie Raitt's definitive version of John Prine's "Angel from Montgomery"—well, hell, the record was on special discount. $5.99, I think, although that was still a lot of jingle in 1978.

If I bought it, I figured while standing there, and saved the rest of my money, *and* scratched up a little extra cash, I could buy two albums the next week. Sighing heavily, I walked to the cash register and saw my grandmother, where she'd been waiting for me to finish shopping. Her jaw hit the counter when she noticed what I was holding. If my wicked-cool Grandma Klein was going to have this response—to an album I had no idea about, except that my beloved "Angel" was on it—what would my snobby Shaker Heights mother think?

———

"She looks like a whore" were the words that fell reflexively from my mom's lips, with equal bits derision and repulsion.

"You're horrible," I returned, flat-toned, refusing to take the bait. "She's made, like, ten records, and she's recorded interesting songs."

"That may be," she volleyed, eyes rolling, "but she *looks* like a *whore*. I can't wait to hear what your father's got to say." My father had recently torn a ratty paperback copy of *Catcher in the Rye* to shreds because of all the swear words it contained. My mother smiled a sour smile, and returned the Marlboro 100 to her Revlon Coral Reef of a mouth.

Undaunted, I raced up to the almost airless, sweltering attic. The moment of truth had arrived. Lifting the arm of my cheap record player, I settled the shiny black disc, picked up the arm with the needle, and held it over the spinning vinyl.

Closing my eyes and hoping I'd not wasted six good dollars, I lowered the arm and felt the stylus catch the groove. The guitar sounded Creedence-like or maybe a little Ike & Tina; there was a yelp, then someone started pumping a kick drum like their life depended on it.

"Lover Good-Bye" was a little more rushed than any Eagles or Linda Ronstadt record I'd ever heard. There was swagger and a brazen quality to the declaration over a nervously buzzing electric guitar, drums pumping like ramped-up anger: "When rain clouds roll, you're gonna get thunder, when lightning flies, it's gonna burn the sky / When lovers lie, you're bound to lose your lady, that's just why I'm telling you good-bye ..."

More blistering than plain tar blacktop, the hinges of hell, or the iron smelters down by the Cuyahoga River, Tucker leaned into the song, tore off words, and spat them out. There was no tentative here. She was sexy as hell, mad as hell—and way the hell over it. After a couple of hard-chugging verses, the electric guitar started picking up its own momentum, circling and winding higher, torquing the tension and ratcheting up the heat.

"I'll turn and walk away, and [snotty laugh] never look back at you ..."

So, *this* is how it *is*.

Going to an all-girl prep school, I found boys to be a mystery and an annoyance. Clumsy, aggressive, fickle, dumb. You never really knew what you were getting—and you were never quite sure what to do with it when you got it. But here was Tanya Tucker, laying it out like letters in the alphabet. A-B-C-D ... DONE!

My word! She looked nothing like anyone I knew, and *did* resemble the working girls picking up johns on the street corners of Prospect and Chester on the fringes of Cleveland proper. But Tanya Tucker knew things, and I wanted to find out about those things.

And if some of the easy-listening stuff—"I'm the Singer, You're the Song," "It's Nice to Be with You"—felt like bad cocktail lounge or early fern bar, "Not Fade Away" had the same roll and boogie that Little Feat was plying—with Mickey Raphael of Willie Nelson's band bleating away on a harmonica and Tucker cheetah-snarling with feral abandon.

There were—heaven help me!—punk guitars stinging "Brown-Eyed Handsome Man," making the Arizona-born Tucker some kinda southwestern C&W kin to my beloved Rachel Sweet. As the piano rose, fell, and slid with full burlesque swerve and bravado, this former mainstream country star seemed to be pouring turpentine over all of what had come before. "If You Feel It," buoyed by a bank of early synthesizers, had the same little-girl brass sound building to pure punk Phil Spector nostalgia, and then the chorus with the gospel-oriented Waters Family providing sanctification.

The closest thing to country was the back-and-forth shuffle "Texas When I Die," with its dry vocals-only opening declaration: "When I die, I may not go to heaven / I don't know if they let cowboys in / If they don't, then just let me go to Texas / Cause Texas is as close as I've been . . ."

As the dobro rode up and braided itself into the melody, this was everything I figured boot stomping must be. Kinda sloganeering, kinda off-key-singalong-inviting. "Texas When I Die" hoists a brew, pledging allegiance to the Lone Star State, bull-riding men, and Willie Nelson songs. Protecting the base: it *was* a country hit.

It was what it was. And it wasn't for me.

But the biggest revelation was Prine's "Angel." Slow, steamy, and slightly dark, there was a foreboding to the track—something that echoed Dann Penn's "Dark End of the Street." When the track fell just slightly behind the beat, the anguish and languish in Tucker's delivery came out, equal parts blues and soul. She wasn't telling a story, she was giving witness—to how life leaves you busted, dreams pass you by, and all you can do is look back and wince, clinging to memories like a life raft.

Slipping through melody, attenuating vocals, pouring on the power in odd places, she sounded like she was singing for her life. Not yet twenty, she'd seen and done much, and had—perhaps—come up emptier than the fairy tale suggested.

I knew just how she felt. Playing golf with women far older than me, listening to them talk about cheating husbands, the tedium of marriage, and who they might've been, I was scared senseless about the fate that awaited me. Hearing Tucker deliver what felt like a combustive eulogy for expectations, I was both uneasy and unsettled by how unabashedly she put it out there.

———

Years later, on a lost late night, John Prine would talk of being summoned to the studio by Tucker to sing harmony on his song. "But I don't know how to sing harmony," he confessed to the tempest in the vocal booth.

"I don't either, just sing it with me," she responded, full of fire and Lord knows what else.

With Tucker's great big bull-ridin' boyfriend sleeping it off on the sofa nearby, Prine broke into a cold sweat as he felt her lean into him—and press him to sing those words he'd written for someone fading away from disinterest. You could hear the wistfulness when he told the story, and one can only wonder what being thigh to thigh with such a molten force of nature might have ignited inside a guy raised on his father's love of Hank Williams Sr.

It raised *my* pulse, listening in the attic of my parents' house, and I had no clue what *any* of it was about. In my knee socks, plaid skirt, and Hanold's white shirt, I was still pondering the moistness in my white cotton panties when slow dancing with boys I didn't even like in the dining room at University School or the gym at Hawken.

This was a lexicon beyond my understanding. But long before Madonna offered her navel as a beacon for the young and the restless, Tucker was sending out a Morse code of heartbeats, carnal thumps, and raw-throated vocals that cut through whatever crossed their path.

Though I would never make the Sandy good-girl-to-bad-girl transition of *Grease*, I would find a brio of my own listening to Tucker throw down. With a turbulent home life of my own, boys my own age held little interest for me—and it wasn't long before I was parking with golf pros and learning how my insides were wired. If Tucker was brash and audacious—capable of serious conjugal carnage—I was still committed to the notion that only one zipper—mine—would be released. But listening to her sh-sh-shaking tumble through "Heartbreak Hotel," I found a resolve to push my nascent sexual boundaries while holding my very Catholic moral line.

———

TNT was Tucker's ninth album. After a long run at Columbia Nashville—produced by Billy Sherrill, the George Jones and Tammy Wynette mastermind—Tucker's move to MCA was meant as a declaration of independence. Having scored seminal—if sexually forward, almost lurid—hits with "Would You Lay with Me (in a Field of Stone)," "What's Your Mama's Name," an untamed take on Helen Reddy's unhinged "Delta Dawn," and a ten-year-old daughter's tale of a father's cuckolding and revenge, "Blood Red and Going Down"—delivering more wide-open wobble than muscular vibrato—Tucker had found a trope that worked.

Those lowdown tales—as well as southern themes—defined the young girl who sounded like a thirty-five-year-old cocktail waitress on the skids. "The Man That Turned My Mama On" was pure gospel witness undertow, even as it surrendered to the notion of running off with the wrong kind of prospect. There were cornpone cautionary tales ("No Man's Land") and wavery hymns to sharecroppers' dreams and the dissolving of prejudice ("I Believe the South's Gonna Rise Again").

None of it moved me; none of it resonated. This despite my family life, long on alcoholism, flagrant infidelity, mental institutions, and pharmaceutical cures that only made things worse as the seventies turned to the eighties—especially for a middle schooler who couldn't keep her letters straight while white-knuckling it through the chaos at home and trying to make sense of it.

Then came *TNT*, an album that fell out of the sky. Tucker was fighting for her life artistically. On this album she set fire to the ingénue, with a voice that tore the truth from the walls like a drunk grabbing the drapes on her way down.

A romance with Glen Campbell was *People* magazine cover fodder, and the breakup gave the tabloids plenty of ammunition to shoot out weekly horror stories. Tucker toured some, but never got traction. What was true, what wasn't true? None of it mattered. The stories churned and burned, and just kept coming. I watched, enthralled, the tumult somehow larger than the suburban nightmare I was enduring. It had nothing to do with music; she was like some tabloid death waiting to happen, and it puzzled me. Especially because the album continued to live on my turntable: a core-shaking declaration of emancipation.

Eventually, an album called *Tear Me Apart*, produced by the white-hot, "of the moment" hitmaker Michael Chapman—who had helmed records for Suzy Quatro, the Sweet, Blondie, and the Knack—arrived. It never connected. Slightly more processed, slightly more hyped-up, it took that new wave/Top 40 tilt and added a bit of Texas roadhouse at its best, but then fell victim to bloated tracks like "San Francisco (Be Sure to Wear Flowers in Your Hair)" and the tame KISS/Alice Cooper ballad "Somebody Must've Loved You Right Last Night," which unravels a cheating husband's morning-after return. Ewwwww . . .

The things we love when we're young often fade to soft-focus, then blur into nothing. Tanya Tucker had a sparkling moment, like a rhinestone in the dust, then was lost to everything rushing at me. Her personal life got bigger, wilder than her music, and I let go of my fascination, her sexuality becoming more of a cautionary tale.

I would never be that much of a libertine, that bold 'n' frisky. I wasn't made that way, and maybe watching from the sidelines, that was okay. Because it made me mindful, made me intentional, instead of making me someone who constantly had to pick up the pieces. Engaged six times, never married; only one one-night stand in all the years of music criticism and late-night bus rides. Watching Tucker, I learned the hard truth about the awful double standard that is applied to women.

Like it or not, the golf pros seemed to be right: "Never say yes, just never say no." It's the thing that compromises you. No matter how smart, pretty, fun, or carnal you are. And once you're branded, well, you're done.

That's what they tell you. But in Tucker's case, there was that voice: all teeth and hunger, she could turn a song inside out, lash it to pieces, and leave it whimpering for mercy, without breaking a sweat. But once she was an object of lust, nobody talked about her music; it was eclipsed by the sideshow gags, peep-show fashion, and squalid gossip.

For real country stars, there will always be gigs—fairs, casinos, and beer joints of a certain size—and gigs mean paying the bills, the road rising and falling before you. And if you do outrun that tabloid death that seems inevitable, there are turns you don't expect.

As a sophomore at the University of Miami covering country music for the *Miami Herald*, I found myself on several record company mailing lists. Music from acts like the Statler Brothers or Exile would arrive, and I would put the CDs in a pile "in case they come to South Florida." Though country was my beat, the Be Stiff punk of Costello, Sweet, and Rockpile remained the undercurrent of my coming-of-age in Cleveland.

Until the day a glitzy new album cover arrived in my mailbox. Tanya Tucker, peroxided blonde mane flying and wearing what looked like a tinfoil merry widow, stared out at me. After fleeing country music for the wilds of West LA and finding that the terrain was less forgiving and that her skill set made her more celebrity than revered vocalist, she had returned to Nashville.

She was not quite chastened, and A&R man Jerry Crutchfield, recognizing the inextinguishable passion in her throat, signed the still-recognizable name to Capitol. The record—*Girls Like Me*—was Nashville's "new country of the moment." Mining work from the soon-to-be award-winning writers Mike Reid and Matraca Berg, as well as rock/pop star Kim Carnes, Tucker found the soul inside the country, absorbing schlock pop and reinventing it as honest emotion.

Like a phoenix rising from the ashes, she proved gossip and bad decisions can't undo a true talent. Making the journey from precocious kid to grown woman, she had learned to control her instrument. She offered up a complex portrait of a woman determined to make her own rules—and to live how she saw fit.

It was stunning. Once again, Tucker clocked me between the eyes. She had tenacity and resolve, the will to not let go of making music—and the ability, perhaps even humility, to accept what could only be a practical decision. Like it or not, she was a country star; in Nashville, her name still shook the rafters. Having sown her musical wild oats, and finding the land to be fallow, she returned to the place where she mattered.

This was a lesson in resilience and surviving blind alleys, holding on through bad times and letting the good stuff catch up. But also knowing that when you do, you must hold on to what sets you apart in order to survive and thrive. It is not a surrender, but a return, with firm conviction, to what you need to be.

———

Banging around the fringes of my hometown, I had felt exiled because of the gossip over my mother marrying my ex-fiancé. College golf was lost to me because of an injured tendon in my hand, and my father was taking on water emotionally. I wasn't meant for the Junior League, as well-intentioned as those young women were, and I was struggling to give up the habit of my ingrained caretaking.

Since the age of eighteen, I had been writing to pay bills and tuition. It was more dignified than stripping; for me, listening to music was more joyous than shedding my clothes to it as the dollars were waved my way. But the arrival of *Girls Like Me* suggested something else: only you can determine when the rumors and whispers win, when a dead end on the highway finally takes you off the road to where you want to be.

Still a little lost, a bit punch-drunk from a series of "now what?" stumbles, I was bucked up by the album. Tucker dug down, brought back the things that mattered from rock & roll, drove her stakes back into country, and began ascending. She shook off any naysaying, threw her shoulders back, and sang with more conviction, gospel fervor, and catch in her tenor than ever before.

I didn't know what I was gonna do, but listening to the cassette's closing track, the damned-if-you-do, damned-if-you-don't teeter-totter of faith-on-the-brink "Still Hold On," in my '73 Mustang, windows down to the Miami humidity and salt air, somehow I knew without knowing that I'd be okay. Sometimes it's just taking the next step that gets you there . . . and step I did.

Tucker went on to win the Country Music Association's coveted Female Vocalist of the Year in 1991. She had gold and platinum albums and a string of chart-toppers, including "I'll Come Back as Another Woman," "My Arms Stay Open All Night," "Just Another Love," "Two Sparrows in a Hurricane," "Strong Enough to Bend," "If It Don't Come Easy," "Don't Go Out" (with the equally soulful T. Graham Brown), and "I Won't Take Less Than Your Love."

Her kind of country was ballsy and honest. She'd seen life, refused to be hard, and regretted nothing—and she brought it all into the vocal booth. When I interviewed her in a cookie-cutter hotel room after her show at a South Florida fair, she was full-tilt and straight-on, asking as many questions about me as she answered about herself—and preaching a gospel of how to live it to tell it.

Emboldened, I kept sending my clips to bigger publications. Tower Records' *Pulse!* put me on the road with Neil Young before his hard-country *Old Ways* was released, then gave me a cover for *The Highwaymen* with Johnny Cash, Waylon Jennings, Kris Kristofferson, and Willie Nelson. The *Cleveland Plain Dealer* started using me, as did *Rock & Soul*; then *SPIN*; then the *Los Angeles Herald-Examiner*, *Musician*, and *BAM*.

Girls like me don't move from hotel suite to hotel suite interviewing Linda Ronstadt, Dolly Parton, and Emmylou Harris, let alone have Harris congratulate them upon graduating from college. Girls like me don't get flown to Wolf Trap in Vienna, Virginia, to interview John Prine for the bio for *German Afternoons*, his second album for his own label. Girls like me don't get boosted out of locked bar windows by maverick comics like Sam Kinison.

But somehow I did all of that, mostly while still being a college undergrad. And like Tucker, once I found a foothold, I just kept climbing. Once you've been down or sidelined, you learn to take nothing for granted. Four years of *Rolling Stone*, freelancing aggressively for the *Los Angeles Times*, a cover of the *Saturday Evening Post*, a spread in *Harper's Bazaar*—it piled up, and I was never ungrateful. Despite being overworked and never having enough time, I always knew there were more records to listen to and bands to see.

Fashion comes and goes; music lasts. In 2016, after an autobiography, a reality show, and more records, Tucker received the Academy of Country Music Cliffie Stone Pioneer Award. It was a moment that marked over four decades of shooting out the lights and having an impact. For a girl like her, what else could there be?

$\mathcal{ele}$

RITA COOLIDGE

———

A Dark-Eyed Cherokee Country Gal

KANDIA CRAZY HORSE

C ountry music—which has also been known as hillbilly, old-time, and country & western—arose from southeast-ern America out of a confluence of African and Native American roots and songs from the British Isles, hybridized in the southern Appalachian Mountains and their environs. The country industry, long centered in Nashville, is exported globally with a white face, and while there has been increasing research on and illumination of the African creation of the banjo and black musicians' influence on the forefathers of the coun-try genre over the past twenty years or so, the Native American strain is scarcely recalled. This is where I come in, a Pamunkey country and Native Americana singer-songwriter, also of Afri-can and Scottish descent, with roots in Virginia's Shenandoah Valley and Daugherty County in southwestern Georgia. I came to be such an artist not merely because of my Dixie heritage and family ties to Georgia-born luminaries of the 1960s folk revival and cultural nationalist circles, but also because I fell under the spell of the iconic, indigenous country-rock songbird Rita Coolidge.

As a radio baby and bluegrass lover born the year that Rita Coolidge met her former husband and musical partner, Kris

Kristofferson, on a flight from Los Angeles to her adopted hometown of Memphis, I grew up in a revolutionary, progressive household wherein music and all the other arts were celebrated— with gospel, folk, country, southern soul, jazz, Motown, and African sounds holding particular sway. Politically, we were extremely attuned to the Black Liberation struggle and the struggles of others in our Third World coalition, including AIM—the American Indian Movement. In those heady days before so many went crazy, while the Vietnam War still raged and the second Wounded Knee went down, and freedom still seemed within our grasp, our soundtrack consisted of music that centered on the twang and the grassroots and that told stories about the simple pastoral life. And looking out into popular culture, beyond the freedom fighters then fetishized by the radical chic cohort, I identified with those women who should have been the huge rock & roll and country stars of the moment—Mavis Staples, Gladys Knight, Millie Jackson—and their red-brown sisters: Buffy Sainte-Marie, Karen Dalton, Cher (who was Armenian, yet famously sang of being a "Half-Breed"), and lovely Rita. They were whom I saw reflected back to me, as a little, rustic-identified, very creative girl of color trying to make sense of a chaotic western civilization in general and America, during its 1960s hangover, in particular.

Hearing or seeing Rita Coolidge duet with my Viking/Texan dream man, Kris Kristofferson—revered by me initially more for his stature in progressive circles as an activist, Rhodes Scholar, and actor than as a country singer—only enhanced my identification with Coolidge, gained from learning that we shared several key biographical traits: we were both born on that high holy witch day, May Day; we are both members of southeastern nations—she's Tsalagi (Cherokee); and we both have Scottish ancestry—her father was a Baptist minister, and I am the granddaughter/niece/cousin of Baptist preachers. And we both heeded the siren call of the Laurel Canyon cosmic country sound.

Rita Coolidge was born near Nashville, in Lafayette, Tennessee, in 1945. As I pen this piece, she is seventy-one, is a two-time Grammy winner and recipient of the Native American Music Lifetime Achievement Award, and has just released her autobiography, *Delta Lady: A Memoir*, while recording her twenty-first solo album and touring. Growing up in Tennessee and Kentucky, she was immersed in a musical environment, singing with her sisters, Priscilla and Linda (paralleling another gifted group of southeastern, mixed-blood kin from the same era—the African/Native American Ronnie Spector and the Ronettes, from Virginia). After attending high school in Nashville, then moving to Florida in her teens, Coolidge attended art school at Florida State University, where she formed a folk group with the wonderfully Dixie-fried name of R. C. and the Moonpies.

Later, as a young aspiring singer, she worked—like many of the members of 1960s/1970s girl groups and pop divas—doing radio station IDs and commercial jingles for Pepper Sound Studios in Memphis. There, she recorded her debut single, "Turn Around and Love You," gaining some regional notice. Coolidge's big break came from encountering husband-and-wife country/soul/rock/gospel duo Delaney and Bonnie Bramlett in Memphis and proceeding to tour with them, getting exposure among the British Invasion royalty who loved the couple and even appearing alongside them in *Vanishing Point*. This is a key moment in Coolidge's career when I began to intersect with her, backfilling the often obscure lore surrounding Delaney Bramlett, the amazing former Ikette Bonnie, and their famous friends as I aged through deep reading, briarpatch-digging, and getting to know several of their Southland-to-Los Angeles sonic colleagues, such as Bobby Jones (who was in the Mad Dogs & Englishmen Space Choir, among his other accomplishments). The freewheeling, freaky-deak ensemble became perhaps my prime influence as an artist and latter-day hippie.

Coolidge's association with the Bramletts led to her singing with and becoming romantically involved with the Master of Space and Time and the Tulsa Sound, Leon Russell—then already a veteran sideman of the Wrecking Crew and innumerable seminal 1960s Los Angeles sessions. He dubbed her the "Delta Lady" via a classic song of the same name (although she has had a tense relationship with that title in subsequent decades), and also wrote his oft-covered standard, "A Song for You," about her. She was also a standout on Joe Cocker's 1970 Mad Dogs & Englishmen tour and in the resulting film, which was organized and largely supplied with players by Russell; Coolidge had a featured spot singing tunes like the song she cowrote with Bonnie Bramlett and Leon, "Superstar."

Among those singers and songwriters associated with Russell's Shelter Records and the Bramletts, who hailed from the Deep South, Tulsa, and Omaha, a unique new blend of country, psych, R&B, and folk was emerging, its sanctified sound being conjured throughout their groupings in Los Angeles, especially in Topanga Canyon, where they overlapped with compatriots such as Space Cowboy Sly Stone, Gram Parsons and his Flying Burrito Brothers, Gene Clark, Taj Mahal and his Rising Sons, the great Kentucky-born country-funk auteurs Jackie DeShannon and Jim Ford, and Michael Nesmith's First National Band.

At the very height of the last gasp of country music being revolutionized in Los Angeles, San Francisco, and desert and beach communities in between during the late sixties and into the seventies, Rita Coolidge was there singing, performing, and even being touted, apocryphally, as the cause of the breakup of that scene's most hallowed supergroup, Crosby, Stills, Nash & Young (listen to Stephen Stills' "Cherokee" and David Crosby's "Cowboy Movie," for starters). Landing a solo contract in 1971 with A&M for a critically acclaimed, self-titled album featuring her on the cover in flawless form (in what came to be codified as the "Cactus Rose" style—long, straight, center-parted hair; denim; and native jewelry), Coolidge was also doing sessions with a list of leading lights, including Stills, fellow Tsalagi rocker Jimi Hendrix, Judee Sill, Dave Mason, Bob Dylan, Eric Clapton, and Duane Allman. In addition, she cowrote the coda of the Clapton hit "Layla," originally known as "Time (Don't Let the World Get in Our Way)" (later recorded by her sister Priscilla). She followed this with the releases of *Nice Feelin'* (1971), *The Lady's Not for Sale* (1972), *Fall Into Spring* (1974), and *It's Only Love* (1975)—all featuring songwriting, playing, and vocal contributions from the LA-centered twang milieu, including Neil Young, Bernie Leadon, and Nash; session stars like Venetta Fields; Guy Clark; and the Dixie Flyers.

Coolidge was considered the perfect embodiment of the "sweet little Indian girl" by a generation of West Coast cosmic cowboys raised on midcentury horse operas and playing cowboys and Indians, as well as emerging longhair country boy stars of southern rock, like Allman and his sonic brother Dickey Betts, who donned electric honky-tonk raiment to finesse their troubled identities as blues-loving southerners who had tuned in/turned on/dropped out while trying to disassociate from the legacies of racism and the predations of the planter class—uneasy riders all. Coolidge's voice sounded clearly through this time of deep social changes and the explosion of progressive country; her (southern) soul and image, and her embrace of her mixed-blood roots, leapt off her album covers and her film appearances (*A Star Is Born*) to resound not just in her home space of Nashville but in Indian country itself.

While other female country and country/rock stars of the period had indelible looks—think Loretta Lynn, Dolly Parton, Barbara Mandrell, Bobbie Gentry, Emmylou Harris, Linda Ronstadt—it was Rita Coolidge's signature 1970s style that you see so painstakingly copied in, and refracted through, hundreds of the coolest outlaw/country–crazy girls' Instagram accounts today (perhaps even exceeding Stevie Nicks' primacy in some arenas)—girls who often have Kristofferson lookalike beaux to match. She appeared as a muted New Mexican Native American paramour of her former husband's outlaw character in Sam Peckinpah's *Pat Garrett and Billy the Kid* (1973), and served as a veejay in the early days of VH1's existence, but Coolidge may be best known for her 1978 platinum smash *Anytime...Anywhere*, which featured R&B hits "(Your Love Keeps Lifting Me) Higher and Higher" (Jackie Wilson), "We're All Alone" (Boz Scaggs), and "The Way You Do the Things You Do" (The Temptations), plus the theme from the 1983 James Bond film *Octopussy*, "All Time High." Yet her lived life, with and without Kristofferson, is characterized by the values and the worldview of a deep-rooted country girl.

As Kristofferson's all-around partner following their marriage, Coolidge was as prominently placed to witness and participate in the birth of the outlaw country movement as Jessi Colter. She also helped usher in the Los Angeles rustic rock sound and scene that begat the Eagles and that, ultimately (via that group and Fleetwood Mac), would come to have an aesthetic stranglehold on post-1990, post–Garth Brooks country as veteran arena rockers flocked to Nashville in the wake of former L.A. singer-songwriters like J. D. Souther and Wendy Waldman to mix it up with suburban-bred hat acts no longer steeped in the old rural verities. (Even now, while acknowledging the prior moves of Hank Williams III, Shooter Jennings, Elizabeth Cook, and Jamey Johnson, we're seeing overt outlaws ride again with the rise of Sturgill Simpson, Whitey Morgan, and the splendidly bearded Chris Stapleton.) Coolidge recorded several albums with Kristofferson, winning Grammy awards for Best Country Vocal by a Duo or Group for their hits "From the Bottle to the Bottom" (1974) and "Lover Please" (1976). While their duets don't tend to be regarded as highly by critics as those of Gram Parsons and Emmylou Harris, Richard and Linda Thompson, Roberta Flack and Donny Hathaway, or Lindsay Buckingham and Stevie Nicks, the Kristofferson/Coolidge duo albums—*Breakaway, Full Moon,* and *Natural Act* (plus his *Jesus Was A Capricorn*)—are always sought after in the record collector circles I move in, and scarcely a month passes in which vintage television footage of the couple singing "Help Me Make It Through the Night" does not circulate on Facebook.

Indeed, social media atomizes Rita Coolidge's image as a country and native ideal, but it's the creative work she continues to do behind that façade that is held most dear. The 1990s and 2000s saw Coolidge turning her sonic focus more fully toward

Indian country, reaching back to her Tsalagi ancestors, who had been forced to walk the Trail of Tears in the 1830s, in company with her late sister Priscilla (formerly the wife and musical partner of Stax legend Booker T. Jones) and her niece Laura Satterfield. They called themselves Walela, named after the Tsalagi word for hummingbird. This is the other storied project of Coolidge's oeuvre that informs the present song-catching work that I do. The songs were collected on *Walela, Walela: Unbearable Love* and a live album. Walela sang on *Music for the Native Americans*, the soundtrack for the TBS series *Native Americans*. Coolidge found a connection with the Band's Robbie Robertson—who is Mohawk, and one of the most revered architects of what is now termed Americana—in addressing the musical void for indigenous music. Walela has illuminated a rich path at a time when there are increasing numbers of younger native, black, and other singer-songwriters of color in the United States and Canada seeking to gain creative and commercial parity in the country and Americana genres while retaining traditional elements. Coolidge's voice remains husky-sweet and pure, not characterized by the vocal gymnastics of the post–Whitney Houston "oversouling" era we're still mired in. She has said of her music, "any time the spirit is speaking through the music, that's soul in a very pure sense of the word." This sentiment, and her muse myth, infused my mind when I wrote my own ode to Buffalo Springfield and Laurel/Topanga, "Quartz Hill" (echoing Stephen Stills's lyrical homage to Rita Coolidge, "Cherokee"):

> *The dark eyed Cherokee*
> *Like the raven she knows me*
> *The secret she keeps like her soul so deep*
> *Nothin' 'round here gets to me*
> *Like the lady from Tennessee*
> *Like the lady from Tennessee*

After being raised as a girl full of wanderlust in Africa, from the Sahel (where I internalized proto-Imazighen desert rock

á la Tinariwen and Bombino, even as I cleaved to my Crosby,
Stills & Nash cassettes) to Maseru-in-the-Mountains, to Accra
on the Bight of Benin, I spent a decade based in Manhattan
and Hot'lanta, adventuring upon, and then covering as a rock
critic, the 1990s southern rock renaissance. My own Lady of
the Canyon moment began when I finally arrived in the City of
the Angels at age twenty-nine to hang out with former canyon
elders, great musicians like my play-uncle Bobby Jones of Delaney Bramlett's circle. There I connected in sound and social
gatherings with the then-embryonic reflowering of the Laurel Canyon music scene via southern migrants who tended to
befriend a favored band, Beachwood Sparks, or to sneak slyly
into becoming moneyed rock stars as so-called freak-folk wor-
shippers of Linda Perhacs and Vashti Bunyan. I enjoyed a flash
of gnosis listening to Ramblin' Jack Elliott talk about Alabama-
born Odetta as a canyon lady, since my dear, late mother, Anne
Marie, had long wished for me to model myself on the "Queen of
American folk music." Although I was too African and perhaps
too self-realized—as seen in the feathered adornment of my
very long locks and innate skill in draping my curves with vintage calico and Indian prints—to become a muse to any aspiring
players in that self-conscious and racially segregated scene, I
did find myself, during those early years, in a partial "Cowboy
Movie" scenario (though I did not cause any bands to implode,
just as Rita Coolidge can never be blamed for what very gifted,
rich, entitled, egomaniacal rock stars elected to do).

Inspired to sing and write songs by the decree of my sistah
gal, former Virginia-homesteader-turned-Sunset-Beach-surfer
Jennifer Herrema (Royal Trux, Black Bananas), I found my
voice somewhere between Bakersfield and Bolinas. I obsessed
over the Kentuckian twang of *Harlan County* auteur Jim Ford
and *Laurel Canyon* auteur Jackie DeShannon. I quietly composed what would come to be my *Stampede* song cycle—yes,
comprising a nod to the mythic lost Buffalo Springfield album
but, even more, signifying my surname and the emotional
effects of the season of loss that had conjured the songs—and

I spent some quality time with the newly crowned "King of Laurel Canyon," who hailed from North Carolina, talkin' 'bout his main man Graham Nash, Gram Parsons, my most beloved Gene Clark, and others among our fellow southerners who had transitioned to California easy-rock freedom in the 1960s and 1970s and become global icons. I played the Grand Ole Echo in Austin, Texas—an L.A.-born annual live music showcase founded by my dear friend Kim Grant—and watched successive waves of guitar-toting young women decamp for the Coast in the hope of being framed like Joni Mitchell in the canyon with her dulcimer (in a photo by my main man Henry Diltz, who also took the original cover image for my album *Stampede*). The current Coastopia is nowhere near as starry-eyed as it was in that mid-century era, yet young country-rockin' pickers who cannot yet afford Nudie suits still prop up the bar at the Troubadour, and the girls who love and feed them take pains to channel Rita Coolidge. I learned the hard way—with beautiful Rita and Buffy Sainte-Marie and Karen Dalton effigies perched on my lacy shoulders—that you have to speak truth to power in your own songs and hold on to your woman's agency even in the ghost notes, because these singing cowboys of hip precincts like Laurel Canyon are oftener than not composing odes to girls they never even met, let alone slept with. A flesh-and-blood damsel-in-distressed cutoff jeans, as I sing of in a tune from my sophomore effort *Canyons*, "Scene & Herd," cannot compete with The Myth.

As I have spent this year assembling a new band, Cactus Rose, with members from my New York City Native American circle, and completing a huge backlog of songs for my third album, also called *Cactus Rose* and featuring more woman-centered tales of spirit-weaving and navigating the New West and negotiating romance with the day's self-appointed heirs of Gram Parson, Kris Kristofferson, and Townes Van Zandt, I marvel at Rita Coolidge wrestling the demons of the "Delta Lady" title while penning her memoir. I write themes for imaginary Westerns and muse on how to get out alive. Being in the midst of a 1970s outlaw country revival, in terms of self-fashioning, gestures, and sonic references, it is fascinating to see these past histories regenerated and lifestyle choices repeated without a good deal of trepidation; do they not heed Waylon, or listen to Tompall Glaser and his brothers' "Wicked California"? As one of the Native American Seventh Generation, and a twang singer-songwriter from Indian Country, my focus is on not the "lonesome cowboys [that] are turned on in Tinsel Town" (about which Leon Russell once famously sang) but rather the deep source of southern soul that persists in this rich genre despite the predations of jaded purveyors. And with my "cowgirl movie" compositions, imbued with ritual and rite, I am interested in who defines "Americana" now that it's a *Billboard* category, fully aware that there has been a longtime problematic engagement with artists of color in that sphere. Seasons, they change, but some of us are the true rightful carriers of the Changing Same. I prepare to take up that hallowed African instrument, the banjo, and continue to songcatch, seeking to conjure the Mystic beyond the Mythic, honoring my mother in the Spirit World and all of my Ancestors before me— and, dark-eyed Tsalagi country girl Rita Coolidge, I *see* you.

LINDA RONSTADT

Canciones de Corazón Salvaje

GRACE POTTER

I remember the first time I saw a Linda Ronstadt record cover. I was six years old, and it was a beautiful picture of her. She was in a bathrobe, and she was sitting in front of a mirror. She looked so beautiful with her hair up, and some of it falling down.

There was a real elegance to it. I didn't know what the music was, just that I wanted to listen to it. Whatever that music might be.

It would've been 1989. My mom had all our records in this one room. It was the biggest room in the whole house, and the entire record collection was across one entire wall. There was a fireplace, and there were two totally broken-in chairs, and there was always someone, it seemed, lying on the sofa, just listening to music.

My parents were artists, and they needed all that music. They had a company called Dream On Productions, and they'd take all these pictures of downhill skiing, crazy festivals, and Viking cruises, and set them to music, then show them in town. Like happenings. Or they'd use the records for project presentations.

The classical and sound effects records they kept up high, because they were expensive. But I listened to everything I could reach. My mom had a whole section of women rockers: Emmy-lou Harris, Bonnie Raitt, Stevie Nicks—and Linda Ronstadt.

I thought it was so strange: why are all the girls in one place? But now I realize there's a femininity to rock & roll that's so different. There's a softness and mystery, even when it rocks ... and it pulls you in in a completely different way. As women, we have more tenderness in our hearts and our minds.

Every piece of music I've ever written, I've seen first. I would only listen to records because of the way the covers looked to me. And it was the same with Linda Ronstadt. The images of her are so compelling, she's so powerful and dynamic visually; then, the quality of her voice is so welcoming, it draws you in—pulls you, almost.

So I remember looking at that album—*Simple Dreams*—and wondering, "How is this going to translate into a story?" And you could just *feel* it, *all* of it. "Blue Bayou" was always the one for me. Even now, I listen to "Blue Bayou" when I'm having a shitty day ... I listen to it when I have to go into a crappy conversation or a really intense meeting. It's my total comfort food, and it makes me feel better.

The sadness and the ache in her voice? The way she does it, you get pulled inside *all* that emotion. Listening back then, I felt like I was her *or* I was the lover who was waiting for her. I didn't really understand what that all was, but I felt it.

You have to understand: for all the mayhem I created as a child, I was also very quiet—my sister was the performer. She was the one always walking into a room and casting the roles for a play that evening. She was the real ballerina; I was the one wearing a dude jacket and knee socks and roller skates or red moon boots, something red or pink on top, maybe a leotard with a sweatshirt over it—and a tutu, over all that, that just stuck out.

So, the record where Linda had the roller skates on, *Livin' in the USA*—I could see myself in it. I loved being a little girl, but I was a tomboy, and Linda seemed like that, too. She was real that way. And *Silk Purse*: in that photo, she reminded me of my friend

Georgia Van Trapp. She looked like a little girl, and I was a little girl ... and it caught my imagination.

And there were so many looks! *Hand Grown, Hand Sown*, with the white-fringe piano shawl dress, or that *Linda Ronstadt & the Stone Poneys* record, where, from far away, I used to think it was Neil Young. Then later, there was *Hasten Down the Wind*, with her on the beach with the hat falling behind her, or the Mom Lebowski cover of *Get Closer*. Or the cover of one of the compilation records, the black-and-white picture with her flashing her middle finger! It was *all* fantastic.

What a random and rare situation to come to records that way, but then have the music inside pay off. She was a woman and a singer, presenting her beautiful interpretations of these songs. Just being herself. She changed a lot with her image and her packaging, but it was *always* about representing her music. People really liked it. They responded to all those pieces of her and her emotions.

By the time I was seven, I had listened to everything in my parents' record collection, everything I could get my hands on. But the first time I consumed an artist's complete catalog, it was Linda's—lying on the floor of that great big room, holding those covers in my hands. I remember thinking, "This is a true and believable artist," and experiencing those songs. They led me to so many places.

By the time I was twelve, I knew I'd get more attention being a singer than being a painter or a dancer, but I still tried those things. I wanted to make something you could hold or show ... and songs just faded away. That was a hard reality for me; I had thought I could do anything, had watched my sister and parents have an amazing effect on other people with their paintings.

When I was older still, I did the weekend/overnight thing at Vassar to feel what it would be like to go to college there. And it was awesome, but the music was too deep inside me by then. I had already played my first concert, a benefit for ovarian cancer at the Round Barn. I played Bonnie Raitt, Joni Mitchell, Shawn Colvin. I didn't play "Blue Bayou"—didn't play the heartbeat of my truest influence, because I was afraid people would see right through me . . . It's hard to wear your heart on your sleeve and admit that, because *nobody* wants to be unoriginal.

Now listening to her records, I feel they're invitations to an internal world. And the most beautiful thing about her singing is, she finds that break in her voice, in her vocal, that no one else would have thought of. It seems to happen so naturally. It's so emotional, and it milks the context even more than the words or the chord change.

She has this transcendence. Listening to her songs, I try to figure out what I love about them. I want to emulate the sound and the vibe, to bring those things forward. That's why she's inspirational to me: for the feelings and intentions behind the songs. And when she's serving as this amazing filter—singing someone else's song—she never takes away from the writer, but reaffirms their nuances, makes them more magical.

And I love the fact that Linda Ronstadt dresses sexy. She's not trashy, and she's cool. The hip-hugger tight jeans and the bell-sleeve silk shirts . . . It wasn't conscious, but looking back on all those images now, I realize that I did a whole tour dressed just like that!

She has this whimsy, and she's theatrical. She can dive into a look, have fun with it. On *Canciones de mi Padre*, she's not in costume: that's her heritage. And it looks amazing. So natural and comfortable—for a half-German, half-Mexican girl from Arizona, those songs and the clothes are just an expression of who she is.

When she describes mariachi music as the country music of Mexico, it makes sense. When she got to LA, she gravitated to that sound, to the steel guitars and players like Bernie Leadon and Sneaky Pete. Country music was being recontextualized by David Geffen; it was already shifting into the music of Laurel Canyon and Gram Parsons.

Being country isn't about radio, or even your influences. Every time I open my mouth, I'm amazed at what comes out.

I sang "Friend of the Devil" and thought, "Oh, my God! I *am* a country singer!," even though I'm a girl from New Hampshire. It's what's inside of the music that comes out: the emotions and the catch. Linda Ronstadt taught me that, and taught me to be true to those things.

It's amazing to see her try *everything*. She's done standards, and the folk stuff, those Mexican songs, new wave. She finds herself over and over again, and she makes it all seem effortless and feminine and real. She's never a baby doll, either, always a goddess. It comes from deep down inside her.

When I started to write this piece, I researched Linda Ronstadt. I found out about her grandfather, who has seven hundred patents. I saw what a beautiful family they have. Every farmer in southern Arizona took his tractors to Ronstadt's Hardware to be fixed. And all the Ronstadt windmills you see in Tuscon—you didn't know they were her people. But she's so very much of the earth and the elements . . .

By just being herself, she draws people together. Peggy, my mom, *loves* Linda Ronstadt, but partly it's for what she is to *me*: the person who exposed me to music in such a passionate and intimate way. My mother loves the way I responded to it.

I could go on and on about Linda Ronstadt. All the great songwriters—from Elvis Costello to Ry Cooder, from Hank Williams to Neil Young—that she drew on, how seamlessly she interpreted them. How Eric, my boyfriend, didn't realize she didn't write a lot of the songs she sings. And how, when I get up to sing, I hope I have even a small portion of the impact on other people that she has had on me.

When all the entertainment in the world is at my fingertips, all I want to do is go back to my record player and those albums. I want to know that the drummer actually hit the high hat and the toms, that a human being actually touched the instruments. She taught me that: about the humanity above all, and the emotion in the playing and singing.

By the time I was old enough to go see her perform, it was too late; she retired in 2009. So we're going to meet for the first time when I sing at a show honoring her, along with Jackson Browne. I bet I would have loved her concerts, but it doesn't matter. I love her for everything she is—and everything she reminds me to be on my journey.

ell

ROSANNE CASH

———

Expectations and Letting Go

DEBORAH SPRAGUE

People have expectations. And people are subject to the expectations of others. Anyone who's had those two realities dovetail peacefully and perfectly is really lucky—or lying to herself.

It certainly didn't happen for me: as the only child of a single mom who eked out a living as a secretary at a construction company, I wasn't supposed to make it out of my working-class, inner-city neighborhood. I wasn't supposed to become an art-damaged outsider before I even reached middle school.

I wasn't supposed to be transgender.

But we're getting ahead of ourselves here—it would be years, decades even, before I came to terms with my true self in any practical way. It was never far from the surface, mind you: always bubbling under in my psyche and, now that I look back at it, never all that far below the surface in my physical presentation.

Expectations for me were pretty simple, in the global sense. Stick around school, stick around the neighborhood, go work in one of the factories that employed everyone else in the family, and start pumping out enough kids to fill up a house. Fortunately, my mom thought a bit differently and tossed a wrench into that machine—by encouraging me to become the first in the family to go to college, if not actually insisting that I do so (and then, likely as not, to fulfill the rest of those obligations).

Though I didn't know it way back in my adolescence, Rosanne Cash and I had a lot in common when it came to expectations. She wasn't an only child, but she was the golden child—the eldest, the one who, it was abundantly clear, could carry on a legacy. Strike that: *must* carry on a legacy. Her crib was, metaphorically—sometimes literally—set up in the hallowed halls of Sun Records, where her dad recorded his first sides as she wailed along (off microphone, of course).

I knew all about those Cash sides from the time I was in diapers, thanks to a childless aunt and uncle who adored vintage country. They inundated me with the gospel according to Reds Foley and Sovine, whom I grew to find kinda corny in my precocious snottiness, but they also introduced me to the Man in Black, who was indelibly cool to just about anyone who encountered him—even a deeply conflicted budding rebel with a propensity for acting out and getting suspended from school, and who developed an early fondness for weed—all to keep that gender "thing" at bay.

Rosanne Cash had a very different set of borders to push when she was entering adolescence. Yes, she existed in something of a fishbowl as the daughter of a celebrity, but mere visibility was the least of her concerns, as she would tell me decades later, in the late 1990s. Watching her father survive on a steady diet of substances far stronger than mere "herbal medicine" was both frightening and numbing. She saw his copious pill-popping as the wrecking ball that ended her parents' marriage, but also as the fuel for the engine of his career—a combination that quashed her desire to follow his artistic path while inexorably pushing her to turn down the same road in terms of substance use.

Early on, Rosanne bowed to expectations. She hit the road with her dad and spent a couple of years playing the good daughter, behind the scenes, then onstage. For a teenager, that was enough. But when she saw an opening, she leapt—landing in various locales around the globe, gaining some traction in Europe, and taking a stab at making L.A. her lady. Eventually she returned to the Nashville confines that served as both hindrance and nurturer.

My own evolution might have been even more circuitous and marked by fits and starts. My move to New York, where I immersed myself in punk rock, then in goth—hey, all the better to slather on the eyeliner and hairspray—led me to realize I had part of the game down pat. But not the part that I wanted to master. That meant another uprooting, this one across country to the left coast, where I encountered Rosanne in person for the first time—not long after I landed my dream job, an editorial position at the magazine that pretty much unilaterally shaped my pop culture aesthetic.

There wasn't a lot of room for Rosanne in *Creem* magazine circa 1988, and she recognized that—but we sat for a good long while, going down rabbit hole after rabbit hole in a chat that ended up, ultimately, being more about her dad than about her. Then again, she did open the door to that by taking on one of his most down-home songs, "Tennessee Flat Top Box."

The patience she showed in that chat probably had a lot to do with the fact that she was at the top of her game, commercially speaking, but it also spoke volumes about her core strength—a strength that she'd soon draw on to step away from . . . well, just about everything, from her marriage to her safe space in Nashville, via a relocation to the Big Apple.

I tried to get away from safe spaces, too, and made my first furtive, under-the-radar attempts at gender transition around the same time. Back in New York, I sought out black-market "mother's little helpers" to speed that process and convinced myself I could stay the course, but ended up retreating back to the shadows, where I'd stay for years to come.

Rosanne spent her fair share of time in the shadows as well, shadows that informed some of the darkest material of her career—notably, the unrelievedly claustrophobic, inward-looking album *The Wheel*. But rather than suffocate in those closed quarters, she opened a window and began the arduous process of granting access to the things that she'd withdrawn from.

As time went on, she was able to exorcise (for lack of a better term) the demons surrounding her relationship with Johnny on the darkly compelling *Black Cadillac* album, a set of compositions that focused almost entirely on the abyss—with Cash diving into the void and emerging both steelier and softer, finally at peace with the complexities of the ties that bind.

With that out of the way, she took on the daunting task of confronting "the list," a litany of songs her father referred to as his very foundation—and, by extension, her own. He'd bequeathed them to her when she was still a callow teenager, but, callow teenagers being what they are, she had tucked the paper away and forgotten about it—until he passed, leaving this one unresolved matter.

These weren't songs that he'd written, but they were songs that served as markers along his personal artistic path, songs that came to be included on an album called *The List*—Rosanne Cash's first-ever "covers" set. Less like gravestones than musical equivalents of the Stations of the Cross, these pieces served as places to stop and reflect, and to gain strength through that meditation. It's telling that *The List* is peppered with songs about longing for, perhaps even achieving, escape—be it from a bad situation, a bad place, or this mortal coil. The picture it paints is of a woman—or, given that the actual list was compiled by her then-septuagenarian father, a man—looking for that crack in the foundation, that open window, that hidden exit.

Upon first listen, it was clear to me that Rosanne wasn't just singing these compositions, she was inhabiting them. From the romantic hangover of "She's Got You" (made famous by Patsy Cline) to the existential desperation of Son House's aching "Motherless Children," she absorbed the source material, then wove a tapestry that shimmered in gorgeous dark colors—a vivid illustration of poet Jalaluddin Rumi's assertion that "sorrow prepares you for joy. It violently sweeps everything out of your house, so that new joy can find space to enter."

The album also allowed Cash and me to cross paths for the first time in a decade. When she walked into our interview studio—about as sterile as an operating room, and usually just as conducive to pleasurable conversation—she registered some memory of our past encounters, but quickly focused on something more in the moment.

"Hey, we're wearing the same nail polish," she said, reaching over to take my hand and turn it toward the window, all the better to examine the color: a dark maroon, by OPI (I can't recall the name right now).

I froze. It was a Monday morning, and I had spent the weekend living, as those in the trans community say, "authentically." It was the very beginning of my transition, and I was taking baby steps, seeing a therapist—the first one I'd ever spoken to—to hash out exactly how I'd be moving forward with my life.

At her suggestion, I began using weekends to test myself, to expand my comfort zone, to live as *me*—a me I had to pack away as neatly as possible before returning to the so-called real world. That meant being sure that all signs of Deb were scrubbed away, and I'd been diligent about getting that right, until this first slip-up.

Cash didn't press the matter, didn't question why a "guy" in this radio conglomerate was rocking her look. But she did—and this still sticks with me—break the typical radio-land interviewer/subject wall by insisting I sit next to her, rather than across from her with an equipment-laden mixing board between us.

That setting allowed her to be more tactile than I expected, patting my hand or touching my arm for emphasis when talking about the intangible connections she felt to this material and how it eventually wound around—like that mythical silver cord—to the spirit of her father.

Whether she knew it or not—my guess is probably not, since she'd been paraded around to dozens of these sessions in the weeks before and after our meeting—Rosanne left me with plenty to think about in the days and weeks that followed.

For starters, she gave me new perspective on a slew of songs that I'd known—and mostly loved—for decades.

But the thing that really stuck with me was her attitude toward how she was perceived. How she was perceived by people who really cared about her, and how she was perceived by those who had just a passing interest in her, but who still felt a sense of ownership. You know, the casual fan, the bulk of the following of most artists and the bane of their existence—the "shut up and play my favorite song already" crew.

Those people exist in all of our lives, to some degree. We have our blood relations, and we have our chosen "family" of close friends, confidantes, and loved ones. And then there's, well, everyone else—the boss, the landlord, the neighbor, the folks we're inexorably tethered to, sometimes indebted to, whose opinions we internalize and give equal weight to.

My therapist, Kit, was dogged in trying to break me of that habit. In her words, "5 percent of the people you know casually will be dead set against you transitioning, and 5 percent will be totally on board." The other 90 percent? "They don't give you a second thought once you're out of their sight."

Rosanne's math was slightly different, but the sympathies she shared with me were essentially the same. Hammering home what had become something of a mantra for her in the new millennium, she compartmentalized her following neatly, with a combination of resignation and jut-jawed determination—explaining that she had come to believe she no longer had to be everything to everyone.

She decided to heed one of her own confidantes—without identifying that person—and accept that what really mattered was "the 6 percent."

That, by her estimation, was the rough head count of those who were really on board for her journey—those willing to hop on and go wherever the road might take them, not merely to check in at the standard attractions. So while she was willing to swing by "Seven Year Ache" and any number of the other hits that made her a chart fixture in her own right, she resolved to focus her real energies on her own passions.

"I would look out at audiences and know that some people were there because they wanted to hear the songs they knew," she said. "There were still a few people who were there because they knew my dad, or they knew June, or they saw [*Walk the Line*]. And most of the time, I'd look out and see that they were bored when I would do anything sort of off the beaten path.

"So when I was doing what I was most passionate about, I would see these people who looked totally bored, eyes glazed over, looking around and waiting for me to get back to someplace where they were comfortable. We were never going to find common ground."

When she came to that realization, Rosanne Cash freed herself. She gave herself permission to move on, to put aside her past—distant and inborn as well as recent and self-created. That didn't mean consigning that past to the fire pit, though. It didn't mean viewing earlier years, earlier decisions, through a prism of regret—it meant moving forward, consequences be damned.

And, truthfully, disregarding consequences is the only way to move forward. Trust me.

ele

THE JUDDS

Comfort Far from Home

COURTNEY E. SMITH

T he first and only Judds album I bought was their 1987
Greatest Hits, in a record store in New York City. I was
there on a school field trip in the eighth grade, from a
small town outside Houston, Texas, where there were more
country stations on the radio than pop, and where the school's
spring break was always aligned with the county fair so that kids
could show and sell the animals they raised. I don't know why I
picked up that album in particular at that time and place. Maybe
it felt like a little bit of home to me in a place where I felt utterly
out of my element.

Whatever I was thinking, it was an odd choice for me in 1992,
when the world was being taken over by grunge and Guns N'
Roses, and my music obsessions were deliciously mainstream
pop: Wilson Phillips, Paula Abdul, Mariah Carey, the Bangles,
and Alanis Morissette. But I put that *Greatest Hits* in the bat-
tery-hog CD Walkman I took with me everywhere—a precursor
to how life with an iPod would be—and began listening to the
album every night for the rest of the trip. The soothing feeling
of familiarity it brought me drew me in and lulled me to sleep,
despite my nervous excitement at being in such a completely
alien place.

The Judds remind me of a simpler time, both in my own life and in the world at large, with their small-town, storytelling lyrics. Their debut album came out when I was five, in 1983, and they were well on the way to being country superstars by the time I was eight. Naomi and Wynonna, a mother-daughter duo from Kentucky, would earn a career-spanning fourteen number-one singles and sell over 20 million albums, and they remain one of the most popular duo acts in the history of the genre. They are complete opposites, with Naomi the zany, ladylike one whom everyone wants to befriend and Wynonna the at-first-shy-but-when-you-get-to-know-her-still-shy but stubborn one with an old soul and a deep hatred of sequins, feathers, and all things showy. Wynonna was the powerhouse, with a voice that could bring the roof down, and Naomi had the songwriting chops and an amazing ability to harmonize.

On their mid-eighties album covers, they dressed the same, in fluffy angora sweaters, with that same feathered hair that was the fashion; by the late eighties you could see their two looks diverging, as Wynonna came into her own and embraced a more masculine, outlaw look (though always keeping that long red hair), while Naomi verged off into a style that could only be described as reminiscent of a fifties housewife. Their differences play off each other, making them uniquely who they are. It's the differences, and the disputes those differences cause, that make them so charismatic both on records and in live performances. Only family members could embrace and overcome such a wide stylistic gulf. But this family could only do it for about a decade: the Judds called it quits in the early nineties. Wynonna launched a solo career, while Naomi took some time away from performing following a diagnosis of chronic hepatitis C. Their 1991 Farewell Tour wasn't even the first farewell performance they'd give in that decade, but more on that later.

Listening to the Judds' singles always takes me back to the place I first heard many of them, in the tiny lakeside town where my grandparents lived. My parents didn't listen to country, preferring rock instead, but my grandparents did, and it seemed to be everywhere I went in their little community: at the craw-fish boils and barbecue cookoffs, the Fourth of July fireworks-watching parties and Halloween hayrides. Country songs blared from every pickup truck and honky-tonk I came near, and made up the 8-track collection in my grandparents' back room to which my cousins and I would sing along. My grandparents owned the town's hardware/general store (the town wasn't big enough for its own grocery store), where I spent many hours sitting at the counter and listening to country music when it was too hot to go outside to play. That was almost surely where I heard "Rockin' with the Rhythm of the Rain" for the first time, as well as the one-hundredth time. It still makes me tap my foot. Whenever I hear "Grandpa (Tell Me About the Good Old Days)," I think of my own grandfather—the way his hugs felt, how he smelled, and the way he had of being gruff but tender at the same time. He wasn't big on talking about the good old days, but he surely did laugh when someone told a good story about them. He especially liked the embarrassing ones.

But the song that really sticks with me is "Have Mercy." It's got one of those catchy riffs you can start hearing in your head from just thinking about the title. The lyrics dig into that coun-try music tradition of telling a universal story in a granular way, like when Wynonna mentions that the color of her lipstick is "pink rosé," and knows her man is cheating because he's playing "Haggard and Jones." Dropping names like that is a dog whistle to see if you're a real country fan, one who knows that she means Merle (whom the Judds opened for early in their career) and George (who's considered perhaps the greatest country singer of all time), two of the greatest storyteller/philanderers in the game. That moment when her voice digs into her lower regis-ter—and Wynonna turns from a girl done wrong into a growling, pissed-off, grown woman—is absolute fire.

That change in inflection taught me something about being a woman: it planted the seed of an idea in me that I didn't have to put up with crap, from boys or anybody—and that it was okay to make it known, both overtly and subtly, that I wasn't going to.

There are a lot of moments like that in Wynonna's singing style and in Naomi's harmonies. Truly, the importance of their presence in popular music and the impact it has had on shaping how women feel: that can't be overstated.

As I got older, my consumption of country music shifted from something that was done in a community to something I did in my car, alone. The part of Texas I lived in had so many country stations that you had to have at least one or two in the mix, no matter what your musical preference was, if you wanted to fill all your car radio presets. So, for me, the songs of the Judds were sprinkled in between those of Snoop Dogg and Soundgarden back then.

Over time, I stopped visiting my grandparents on the weekends in favor of driving to every football game our high school team played. There really wasn't any other choice, because it was what everyone I knew was doing. The community revolved around the football schedule, and kids who didn't play football (which was all of the girls) had to choose the way they would support the team: as a cheerleader, as a member of the band or drill team, or sitting in the stands. Being deemed not acceptable as a dancer and not popular enough to be a cheerleader, I was in the band. But, in a fit of practicality, I did decide to become a twirler to avoid wearing the thick wool suits and stupid-looking hats the band members donned, starting in August, in favor of a leotard and some sequins. Naomi Judd would have approved. Being hit in the head by a baton while I learned how to spin around in a circle and catch it was a price I was happy to pay.

Our entire high school hierarchy flowed down from the football players. That old adage that football is a religion proved to be true, and I found myself living in a real-life *Friday Night Lights* right there in my tiny hometown. It chafed me, not only to have to build my social life around this sport I didn't particularly care about but also to feel that I was expected to build an identity, as I became a woman, around what these particular dudes thought was attractive and proper female behavior.

I had that same fish-out-of water feeling that going on my

school trip to New York City had given me. I didn't want to be how these guys wanted me to be, but being a teenager, I also didn't want to be different. Looking back, I can see how those Judds singles that I slipped on like a comfortable blanket during that trip helped me carve out my own ideas of what a woman could be. That Naomi and Wynonna were so different, but still from the same bloodline, spawned the idea that there could be many aspects to a person. I could be that sweet, traditional girly girl like Naomi when I wanted to, or I could be that over-the-top, sequins-wearing, attention-getting version of her. Or I could be an introvert like Wynonna, as well as someone with a definitive, strong point of view, like hers. There could be a time in the world that wasn't about football games and keggers in a field, like the night the Judds praise in "Girls Night Out." I could be the bad guy in a relationship, like in "Change of Heart"—the *woman* could change her mind about what she wanted. I could be sappy and enjoy the endless optimism of "Love Is Alive," or feel just as great singing about dejected lows in "Why Not Me."

I moved away from listening to country for most of my twenties. My college years were dedicated to emo and alternative music, and I took a deep dive into indie rock as I started my first job at MTV in New York City. But when I moved back to Texas in my mid-thirties, San Antonio, to be exact, I found myself back in a world where country music mattered, and listening to some of the new women in the genre as well as revisiting old favorites seemed like coming home in a whole new way.

When I listened to "Why Not Me" for the first time in probably a decade after getting my first Spotify account, I still felt that same old longing the song's opening steel-guitar chords have always brought out in my heart. Singing along to the growl in "Give a Little Love" still made me smile. Trying to hit all Wynonna's notes on "Change of Heart" was still a fun car karaoke game. I guess you could say the Judds are part of my good old past. But with the beauty of their free-spirited, feminine, feminist ways, they are part of my good new future, too.

ele

K.D. LANG

Flawless, Fearless

KELLY McCARTNEY

I t wasn't the first time I heard k.d. lang's voice that carved out a forever place for her in my heart. It was the first time I saw a photo of her, for, in it, I saw a reflection of who I was or, more likely, who I wanted to be. It was 1990, maybe 1991, and media representation of those of us who are "masculine-of-center" was sparse, at best. But there was k.d., handsome and heartfelt, staking a claim for all of us . . . even those of us still nestled safely in our closets.

Actually, in 1991, k.d. wasn't out yet, either. Not publicly, at least. She had released _Friday Dance Promenade_ (1983), _A Truly Western Experience_ (1984), and _Angel with a Lariat_ (1987); recorded a Grammy-winning duet of "Crying" with Roy Orbison (1987); performed at the Winter Olympics (1988); released _Shadowland_ (1988); and won another Grammy for _Absolute Torch and Twang_ (1989), all of which rightly endeared her to lovers of classic country crooners like Patsy Cline and Kitty Wells.

Musically, k.d. put her reverence and respect for the form and its icons at center stage—her first band was called the Reclines, after all. But, stylistically, she injected a sharp wit and a cowpunk ethos into her earliest works, much of which she learned from another country legend, Minnie Pearl. On those first few albums, k.d. still considered herself to be a performance artist, playing with gender by sporting a crew cut while donning a cowgirl skirt and horn-rimmed glasses. By the late eighties, her look had settled into that of a tomboy version of a cowgirl, letting denim, boots, and short hair frame her prairie-born good looks.

Because her talent was undeniable—and she wasn't yet waving a rainbow flag—country music fans could abide by their own version of "don't ask, don't tell" and just enjoy her utterly stunning voice. Heck, Patsy Cline's beloved producer, Owen Bradley, helmed *Shadowland* and recruited Kitty Wells, Loretta Lynn, and Brenda Lee to sing on it. Doesn't get much more classic country than that.

But then, in 1990, the avowed vegan caused an uproar among said classic country folk for appearing in a "Meat Stinks" ad for PETA, earning herself a lifetime ban from country radio. A sign proclaiming Consort, Alberta, to be the "Home of k.d. lang" was even burned in effigy. Naturally, k.d. was bothered by it all, but she never wavered from her convictions. Instead, she doubled down.

Within a couple of months of that kerfuffle, k.d. was waltzing toward the adult contemporary music space with a contribution to the *Red Hot + Blue* Cole Porter tribute compilation benefitting AIDS research and relief. Her performance of "So in Love" was a highlight of the platinum-selling album, showcasing her extraordinary gift as an interpreter of song. She completed her transition in March of 1992 with the absolutely captivating collection that is *Ingenue*. Flourishes of pedal steel here and there were, really, the last remaining vestiges of country music in k.d.'s sound.

In June of 1992, before "Constant Craving" led the album to multiplatinum sales and a third Grammy Award, k.d. came out as gay in *The Advocate*, confirming the open secret that everyone already knew but dared not speak. That year—along with the Indigo Girls—k.d. made a bigger impact on my life, with her courage and conviction, artistry and activism, than anyone before or since.

I still remember sitting on the edge of my seat in the first row of the balcony on August 7, 1992, for the entirety of her first-of-two performances at the Universal Amphitheater in Los Angeles. Having already come out, k.d. introduced the gender-play that is "Miss Chateleine" with a comic bit meant to put everyone in the crowd at ease: "There's been something I've been meaning to tell you, something that's been on my chest for quite some time. So I'm just gonna conjure up the gumption and spit it out." [drum roll] "I . . . AM . . . A . . . LLLLLL . . . LAWRENCE WELK FAN!"

The show was one of the best I've ever seen. And it was a *show*: k.d. is not just an incredible singer, she's also a captivating entertainer, paying attention to every detail, from the punchlines to the performances. Summing up his review of the show for the *Los Angeles Times*, Chris Willman wrote, "Even the most die-hard meat industry activist would be hard-pressed not to switch-hit and walk away from this one a closet . . . *LLLLLL-LANG FANATIC*."

Less than a month after that fateful night, I too became an avowed vegan, and, in November, I became an out queer. Doubtful I could've, or would've, done either without having k.d.'s lead to follow, without having her image to reflect. Seeing k.d. stand so gloriously in her truths inspired me to find and live my own. Though I didn't yet have the capacity to understand or accept it, I'd known since I was a kid that I was queer. But growing up in rural Louisiana did more damage than good, where understanding and acceptance were concerned. (Funnily enough, the same could be said of my veganism: of all the left-leaning things in my life—moving to Los Angeles, working with rock stars, being a homo, living in a meditation ashram, and being a vegan—the one thing my southern-born and -bred father could never get a handle on was my not eating meat.)

So when I *finally* saw someone who looked like me, lived like me, and loved like me, I started moving toward the light that she was shining. Turning toward that light meant turning into myself—digging into my own identity and drumming up my own courage. That process of discovery, sparked almost entirely by k.d., uncovered who I was at my core . . . and who I continue to be today: an Eastern philosophy–abiding, activist-minded queer who works in music and doesn't eat meat.

k.d. continued to shine lights and blaze trails from there on out: having Cindy Crawford shave her in a barber's chair while she leans against her on a 1993 *Vanity Fair* cover is the stuff of legends (and of dreams, if I'm being honest). Wearing a jacket emblazoned with "HOMO" for the 1995 VH1 Fashion Awards is right up there, too. Though I had long copied her style, the extent to which I emulated her, consciously and not, became crystal clear when for Christmas that year a dear friend gave me a sweatshirt embroidered with "HOMO."

In 1993, she and her long-time co-writer, Ben Mink, were working on the soundtrack for *Even Cowgirls Get the Blues*, and I was buddies with their engineer, Marc Ramaer. Knowing I was a huge fan, Marc invited me to come hang with them at Dave Stewart's studio, and then again at Skip Saylor's. I jumped at the chance, not knowing whether k.d. would even be there. The first two times, she wasn't; but that third time really can be a charm.

A friend at k.d.'s label, Warner Bros., had procured for me an *Ingenue* poster, so I showed up and walked into the control room to, once again, find only Marc and Ben plugging away. Then, as we were joking around, the door opened and in strode k.d. I had unfurled the poster so the guys could sign it and she said, "Oh, man. I never liked that photo" (or something pretty close to that). Still, she scratched out an autograph while I decided I should cut my losses and make myself scarce. For whatever reason, I instinctively smiled and winked at her on my way out. How mortifying.

Two years later, the boys were back in town working on *All You Can Eat*, and I got another invitation to hang and hear some tracks while they were being mixed. There I was, twenty-five years old, getting a sneak preview of my hero's new record . . . *again*. At the time, I was working with Vonda Shepard, so I took her along and we invited the guys to her upcoming show at the

Troubadour. They came and, not too long after, I got a call from k.d.'s manager asking me about the drummer (Abe Laboriel Jr.) and bassist (Oneida James) in Vonda's band. Marc and Ben were so impressed, they wanted them to audition for the *All You Can Eat* tour. Neither ended up on that run, but Abe would go on to become one of k.d.'s main collaborators on 2000's *Invincible Summer*. (And, yes, I take a wee bit of credit for that musical matchmaking.)

Because of those very loose ties, that series of records— *Ingenue* through *Invincible Summer*—will always be bound up together in my mind. In them are k.d.'s heartbreak and humility, her vulnerability and her valor, her truth and her triumph. From the wrenching ache of "Save Me" to the quiet confidence of "I Want It All" to the gentle resolve of "Only Love," those albums are filled with songs that serve as signposts on a truly soul-filled journey.

What's more, from 1992 on, k.d. didn't need to use pronouns in her love songs for all of us to know about whom she was singing. And that normalization meant everything to her fans. For better or worse, we knew whom she was dating and we knew when they broke up, so there was no need to highlight the feminine objects of her affection at the potential risk of alienating the wider audience. After all, k.d.'s disarming charm knows no bounds. You can't pin her down or fence her in.

That tabula rasa approach to her art and her audience is the key to k.d.'s universal appeal. She wants men *and* women to be drawn to her in whatever way works for them. When she stood center stage in a three-piece white suit at the 2010 Winter Olympics and sang Leonard Cohen's "Hallelujah," some folks might not have known how to feel about her, but they sure knew how to feel about her voice: there are not many better. As Stephen Holden wrote of a 2004 performance in the *New York Times*, "Few singers command such perfection of pitch. Her voice, at once beautiful and unadorned and softened with a veil of smoke, invariably hits the middle of a note and remains there. She discreetly flaunted her technique, drawing out notes and shading them from sustained cries into softer, vibrato-laden murmurs. She balanced her commitment to the material with humor, projecting a twinkling merriment behind it all."

Even though her music strayed out of the realm of country long ago, every move k.d. has made over the past thirty years has been informed by that original cowpunk ethos that refuses to color inside any lines or rest on any laurels. And that value set doesn't just apply to her music. Somewhere along the way, k.d. turned her spiritual gaze toward Tibetan Buddhism, which sits quite comfortably alongside her animal rights activism, contemplative songwriting, and humanist life approach. While I'm more of a Taoist/Vedantist myself, I have great respect for the deep compassion of the Tibetan Buddhist path, and I count that as yet another intersection between the two of us who have "K" and "D" as our initials.

The past fifteen or so years have seen the release of several more k.d. collections and collaborations, including her 2016 project with Neko Case and Laura Veirs, aptly monikered case/lang/veirs. On August 6, 2016, when their tour brought them to Nashville's Ryman Auditorium—the Mother Church of country music and long-time home of the Grand Ole Opry—k.d. greeted the crowd with a big ol' Minnie Pearl-style "HOOOOOW-DYYYY!," before reminiscing about how she'd been kicked out of the Ryman on several occasions. Both Case and Veirs seemed to understand the gravitas of k.d.'s triumphant return, and everyone else in the room understood it, too, by the end of her rafter-raising cover of Neil Young's "Helpless."

As soon as I heard the song's opening plunks, I let out a big ol' "WHOOP!!!" and moved to the edge of my front-row balcony seat, just as I'd done twenty-four years (minus one day) earlier. And I hung on every note, remembering all that she has meant to me over the passing decades. Quite simply, k.d. lang is one of the greatest singers of any generation, with her flawless pitch and fearless control. She is also one of the greatest influences on my life, with her flawless style and fearless sense of self.

LUCINDA WILLIAMS

Flesh & Ghosts, Dreams + Marrow

LADY GOODMAN

She was the girl at the bar. Lanky, blonde, big eyes that drank everything up: she had a will to know and understand all the things that went on around her. Always a little sad underneath the kindness, always asking how you were and *really* meaning it, she had a voice that sounded a bit like a crow gargling kerosene in a raw wind—and somehow it soothed you rather than set you on edge.

Back then, the Palomino Club in North Hollywood was mostly forgotten, with sodden carpet and a counter—nicked, burned, and tattooed by patrons—that ran longer than the line any of us could've walked. There was an old-school cigarette machine in the back, and yellowing black-and-white pictures on the walls, of Emmylou in a rhinestoned cowgirl outfit; Jerry Lee post-prime but raising hell; Linda Ronstadt in tube socks; and Charlie Rich; and Merle Haggard; and John Conley—behind plexiglass, to remind us of the glory days long gone.

Forgotten was too kind a word for it. Bikers had their corners, punks commandeered it a couple nights a week. Faded once-weres with nothing else to remind them of back when they mattered would check in occasionally to feel as if there was still sparkle. In the low light, it was hard to tell. And Ronnie Mack had his Barn Dance, a weekly come-as-you-are country-leaning variety show à la the once-upon-a-time Louisiana Hayride. Largely populated by eager writers and guitar players looking to make their mark on country post–Steve Earle and Dwight Yoakam, the creative foment offered good fun and better music.

We didn't think it wasn't much of nothing. Screaming Siren rockabilly filly Rosie Flores in her bobbed hair and fringe kicked it up with the house band. Über-producer Pete Anderson, the Detroit blues guitar-slinger who had helmed *The Town South of Bakersfield* compilation and Yoakam's breakout *Guitars, Cadillacs, Etc., Etc.*, would be draped over that cigarette machine in the back. Straight-up country singer Jann Browne, whose few perfect singles almost made it, would bring her classic if radio-friendly music, wearing turquoise boots and a white bolero jacket. Sometime-low-rent-skin-mag pinup with a heart of gold, blues-cum-Wurlitzer country queen Candye Kane would show up, blow up, and play the piano with her 44H assets.

It was Fellini in rhinestones, thick smoke, and a bouncer named Tiny, who was the largest human being I'd ever seen. The cast of characters, the buzzing neon, the naugahyde barstool seats—peeling from sweat, humidity, and nervous fingernails driving into them.

Normal was Jim Lauderdale, scooped up in the backdraft of Dwight Yoakam by Epic Nashville for an album never released; he, the too-nice guy with the Manuel suit. Lauderdale had a guitar player who was even lovelier than he was. Buddy Miller, in his bolo tie and western-cut blazer, had more tone than any guitar player I'd ever heard; he played his heart through his fingers instead of using a whammy bar or a lot of digital gymnastics to make his point. Both Buddy and Jim were friends with the girl at the bar, with the sad in her voice, the bangs that fell across her forehead like a sigh, and the broke-in leather jacket.

Nobody really talked about Lucinda's music, though someone whispered that she'd made a couple albums for Folkways a long time ago. They also didn't talk about, but they whispered about, her divorce from one of the Long Ryders, famously Sid Griffin's band and latter-day progenitors of cowpunk. Griffin was an authority on cosmic country icon Gram Parsons. The divorce seemed to be the tinge that permeated, without drowning, Williams's demeanor.

I was fresh from washing out of Florida, trying to figure out what happened next. The Palomino Club was legendary. I was drawn there by reputation, and the notion that it was a bellwether for what was left of the cowpunk movement, which had spawned Lone Justice, the Blasters, the Knitters, Los Lobos, and the more-punk-than-cowpunk icons, X.

Shabby and rundown, it felt like I did. Not much past twenty, a little disheartened by how unfair life can be, I was trying to keep alive the bubbling joy I felt life deserved. Fired by the daily paper where I'd been an overproducing rock critic; a favorite of Neil Young, amongst many; and set up by a guy who needed my job, I was devastated. All I had was a boyfriend who insisted I move to L.A.—and there I was, in a big city that seemed to overwhelm me at every turn.

The Barn Dance felt like *Friends*, or *Cheers*, or any hometown spot where everybody knows your name. You'd walk in the door to smiles, "hell, yeahs," and back-clapping hugs.

For a lost girl, it felt like a haven. And Lu felt like the kind of girl you'd want to be friends with. Totally in sync, miserable and commiserating, and understanding about how cruel fate was, she was the kind of girlfriend who'd listen and lift you up, and never make you feel like you were being whiny.

I'd run into her at Millie's, the dive diner in Silver Lake where the murky people showed up as morning turned to day. Silver Lake wasn't hip then. I don't think punk god and X founder John Doe had even moved there yet; the neighborhood was still so sketchy that my car was broken into three times in four days. Lu and I were both so broke, we'd split an order of toast and drink our tea. Those mornings, which should've felt like shame on a plate with a blue border circling the edge, thrilled me—because this was L.A., and she was a poet, and we were *living* it!

And unlike so many hopefuls, she didn't push her music or

her dream on you. Didn't make you run away from the self-promotion the desperate often cling to and wield like a club, trying to convince themselves as much as the listener. There was talk about sides cut for CBS Records, sides deemed "too country for rock, too rock for country." Talk, too, about all the labels sniffing around, post–Lone Justice, for some kind of Emmylou elixir—but never a deal coming to the table.

But there she was at the Pal, cheering on Jim Lauderdale. Laughing about something, or nothing, with Buddy Miller. Holding her own on a bar stool, side of her head against her open palm, watching whoever was onstage. Sometimes sitting in with a band that included the upright bass player Dr. John Ciambotti, who was a chiropractor since his days chasing music in the band Clover had faded, and Donald Lindley, with his cockeyed fedora and almost-soldier-boy-like stick work on the drums.

Then came what was known as the "Rough Trade album," released as *Lucinda Williams*. A punk label best known for signing the Smiths didn't just show interest, but straight out offered her a deal. Someone named Robin Hurley—was it a man or a woman? Because how could a man understand songs so blatantly female, no matter the toughness?

Make no mistake, these songs *were* tough—even as they threw themselves down the stairs of desire, loss, rejection, and joy. We knew Lucinda's dad was a teacher, but we didn't know he was the poet Miller Williams. Lines like "Is the night too black, is the wind too rough / Is it at your back, have you had enough?" and "She saved her tips and overtime, and bought an old rusty car / She sold most everything she had to make a brand new start . . ."—she came by them honest.

Honest and real. It felt good when you put the record on, heard a life you were living described with simple eloquence. Realized your mundane *was* poetry, and someone *you* knew was great, just because they were. And just because you knew them, because your lives *were* mundane, that didn't mean there wasn't magic there.

Lucinda Williams was a revelation to me, there in that airless apartment overlooking the reservoir—not even a natural body of water—that gave Silver Lake its name. Draped on a mauve couch, listening to Skip Edwards's Farfisa organ whirling out of the speakers, I would feel the rush of anticipation of "I Just Wanted to See You So Bad" hitting my veins like a drug.

Lucinda Williams moved into the deep yearn tempered with hope that was Sylvia the Waitress's escape from Beaumont, "The Night's Too Long"—followed by the barbed-wire ballad "Abandoned," clearly bulls-eyed at the Long Ryder who rode away, leaving her sunshine-through-moonshine ache attenuated on the long vowels like a clothesline overburdened. Gurf Morlix's twisted guitar took that pain beyond words, wringing out her intentions like an old washrag in dirty water.

The brightness returned—even through the prism of that same damned divorce—in "Big Red Sun Blues," as well as the zydeco retreat to home in Louisiana that was "Crescent City." There were lumbering blues that ground down in the lurching "Changed the Locks," and a hushed, tentative ballad that suggested a return to vulnerability and love, the coo'ed and whispered "Like a Rose."

As a trainwreck girl trying to figure out what happens next, suddenly I didn't feel so isolated in failure, so urgent in needing to have the answers. And listening to "Passionate Kisses," which would go on to win Lu a Grammy for Country Song of the Year by virtue of Mary Chapin Carpenter's hit recording, I knew it was the most empowering feminist anthem *ever*.

Suddenly, asking for what I wanted wasn't pushy. As Williams sang about wanting a bed that didn't hurt her back, having enough to eat, warm clothes, a rock & roll band, time to actually think, and the realization of her desires, it didn't seem like too much. As the final chorus swelled up, with the sixties-style "whoa-oh-oas," she shook off any notion that good girls should be happy with what they're given.

> *Do I want too much*
> *Am I going overboard*

To want that touch
I'll shout it out to the night
Give me what I deserve
'Cause it's my right.

Heck, yeah! If Lucinda could sing it, I could live it.

Knowing people in Nashville, I started making calls, started pushing for these songs. Highway 101's manager heard what I heard in "The Night's Too Long." Who else? Knowing Patty Loveless had already cut Lone Justice's "Don't Toss Us Away," I pressed her producer Tony Brown, the A&R man behind the great '80s credibility scare. Use it or lose it, I urged him, "because this song is every woman listening to country radio—and Highway 101'll kill it."

Brown cowboyed up, recording the Appalachian traditionalist who had blood ties to Loretta Lynn. Loveless understood the pining to get out, to get to somewhere more electric, vital, possible. She wasn't afraid of a line like "Now the music's playin' fast, and they just met / He presses up against her, and his shirt's all soaked with sweat."

Around Hollywood, where Williams played Raji's and the Palomino, word was also getting around. Lucinda Williams suddenly wasn't just the girl at the bar, she was a voice that mattered. The poetry of real life dripped from her lips and fingers, plain language and melodies stained with the blues, with folk, with the lights spilling out of the cracks in beer joint walls.

Tom Petty eventually cut "Changed the Locks." Emmylou Harris recorded "Cresent City." Canadian country-progressives Prairie Oyster did "The Price You Pay." Pretty much anyone who was *anyone* loved Lucinda's record, jockeyed with each other to tell stories of how they knew her—or where they saw her.

But back at the Palomino, she was still Lu. Still singing with Jim Lauderdale and Buddy Miller, still playing with her core band, still the girl who heard our stories and shared our lives. Yes, she was on every critic's list that year, it seemed, from the

Village Voice to *Rolling Stone* to *Tower Pulse* to the *L.A. Times*. But she was still ours—and that's what mattered most.

The music business being as much about musical chairs as it is about quality, she signed a deal with a major label, then lost her key executive to turnover. It would be four years before the equally enchanting *Sweet Old World,* and another six until the watershed *Car Wheels on a Gravel Road* earned Lu her next Grammy.

But through it all—like all of us music business gypsies—she cobbled together a life, figured out how to make art on her terms, moved to Austin, Nashville, and elsewhere, and kept going. She'd appear on compilation albums, play dates, break hearts, capture it all in songs.

When she wrote of coitus and self-pleasuring with frank but exquisite rapture in "Right in Time," the elation of orgasm is transferred to her listener, as is the stab to the gut of the kiss-off "Come On" to the guy who never quite completed the climax. Heated, bristling, awesome. Lucinda!

Lucinda, the star, mascara-smeared, three hours late. Always so sweet, you couldn't hate her. Always chasing a sound or a standard for her records, she drove everyone mad—but the results were hard to quibble with.

Lucinda, the kind of woman who could write about a friend who died from a slow suicide in "Drunken Angel," lament her mother's death in "Mama You Sweet," and somehow cover AC/DC's "It's a Long Way to the Top," and make all of them sound cut from the same cloth. Not rock, not pop, not punk, not country, not blues: American. Americana.

Before Americana was colonized, there was Lucinda. Recycling everything that happened, she was a teacher.

Life moved me from Los Angeles to Nashville, where I became a tracer fish for the far cooler people in California. Working jobs in offices, on the phone, on planes, massaging egos, looking for stories, doing this, and that, and this, I was sometimes writing, sometimes consulting, sometimes running a business out of my house—and for thirty-one months, running a department at a major record label.

It was the coal mines of the music industry. Deep in the belly of the action, where no one knows quite what you do or whether it matters, yet there you are. Soaking it up, taking the abuse. You keep doing the work, because you believe in the music, and the artists, and the dreams.

One day, pissed off at a client and turning out of the parking lot of Pancake Pantry onto Wedgewood—when Nashville was far sleepier than it is now—I called a guy who used to badger me to try writing songs. "You still want to?" I asked. He said, "When?"

Intimidated as hell, I walked into his office two days later, remembering the admonition of Songwriter Hall of Famer Matraca Berg: "The new writers show up, and they bring *nothing.*"

"I have an idea," I offered, "something I've had since I was a kid. A line to get rid of guys at closing time, 'cause I was so far underage: better as a memory. I'm better as a memory than as your girl . . ."

I'd written it in textbook margins and across homework assignments and handouts, tattooing three-ring binders with black ballpoint ink. How to keep a messy moment with a drunken, not-seeing-straight guy from turning into a threat to someone's liquor license: it was common sense, and a little dramatic license. Scooter Carusoe and I turned it into a laundry list of truisms about life through my eyes, a fair warning that was as seductive as it was cautionary.

"My only friends are pirates" referred to the ones who could only steal your heart or your soul, your time or your money— the bad choices women make. But ultimately it was aimed at Keith Richards, the swashbuckling guitarist who had a heart of gold. Somehow, the cautionary note has turned into a startlingly invoked catchphrase for pundits like Matt Dowd of ABC News.

"Built to fade like your favorite song" was a nicer way of addressing the French good-bye, while "Never sure when the truth won't do" serves as a genuine confession of awkward social faltering. All those things—maddening or worse, common or less—were in there, and somehow they embodied so many people's lives.

I remember emailing Cameron Crowe for permission to use the name Lady Goodman. He e-mailed back, asking to hear the song, then said he was good to go, though he clarified that the real Lady Goodman wasn't the Penny Lane character in *Almost Famous* at all.

It didn't matter. It was a name to hide behind, as I scraped the marrow of my life—and offered bits of meat and bone to the cause. Lucinda showed me that: meat and bone, ghosts and flesh, *that's* where the songs are.

Along the way, Lucinda set a whole other standard. She would probably be the twenty-first-century Dylan if she were a boy. But better than that, she's a taut and vibrant woman, emotional and braced, tender and ready to stand her ground. A song warrior, she pushes the melodies, lives like a rocker, and shrieks with happiness when she sees old friends after a long time, sweeping them into a big hug.

It wasn't seamless, wasn't without tears in the fabric or holes in the rug. But like everyone else, Lucinda Williams lived through those things—and made great records because of them. Turned life into art, inspiring day laborers like me to see what art *their* lives might hold.

MARY CHAPIN
CARPENTER

Every Hometown Girl

CYNTHIA SANZ

New Jersey–bred. Ivy League–educated. More flannel shirt than frilly dress. Mary Chapin Carpenter was nothing like the female country artists I'd grown up with. And everything like the woman I was growing up to be.

It was December 1990, and I was driving home to San Antonio after my first year working in New York City. Carpenter's "You Win, Again" was just breaking into radio airplay. It was the first single from her 1990 album *Shooting Straight in the Dark.* And it was all of my twentysomething romantic angst set to music.

> *I'm standing here freezing at a phone booth baby*
> *In the middle of God knows where.*
> *I got one quarter left, your machine picks up*
> *But baby I know you're there*

Just one year earlier, I'd moved halfway across the country to begin work as a staff writer at *People* magazine. Living in the city was fast-paced and exciting. I was going to fabulous parties, interviewing celebrities, and building a life for myself.

But I was also single. And struggling with the dating world in New York City. My on-again/off-again college boyfriend had moved on to marry someone else. Subsequent romances had fizzled soon after they began. Driving home that December, I heard my own life in Carpenter's aching alto.

Once called the patron saint of the single woman, Carpenter brought sensitivity and emotional depth—and a decidedly feminist perspective—to country music in the 1990s. Holding her own amidst that decade's herd of "hat acts," she sang about love and longing with a poet's voice and heart-on-her-sleeve honesty.

> *I can't be right if I'm always wrong*
> *I can't stand up if I'm always kneeling,*
> *At your altar or at your throne,*
> *You could show just a little feeling*
> *For who I am*
> *Baby you win again.*

But the heroines of Carpenter's songs didn't take their heartbreak lying down. They demanded answers and walked away with their pride, if not their hearts, intact. For a generation of women like me, trying to navigate the changing currents of love and career, Carpenter was a sister-in-arms. "She gave her heart away one time, and says that she hasn't seen it since," she sang on "Middle Ground," another cut off *Shooting Straight in the Dark*. "All her single friends are men / She thinks married girls are so damn boring."

Part of Nashville's acclaimed "Class of '89," Carpenter hit the charts with a wave of new traditionalists like Garth Brooks, Clint Black, and Alan Jackson. Country was booming, and its boundaries were being pushed ever outward.

My childhood had been steeped in country music. I'd sung along to Dolly Parton, Crystal Gayle, and Reba on the radio. My family watched *Hee Haw* and *The Porter Waggoner Show* every Sunday. And my high school friends and I had two-stepped through our proms.

But Carpenter was a different kind of country artist. Melodically, her sound was closer to seventies rock and folk music, and her lyrics stayed far from country's blue-collar touchstones. She looked different, too. In a sea of sequins and hairspray, she took the stage in jeans and flannel shirts, like she'd just wandered off one of the Seven Sisters campuses. And she sang about independent women charting their own courses.

Of course, Carpenter was always an unlikely country star. The daughter of a *Life* magazine exec, she had gone to prep school, lived in Tokyo while her father was working abroad, and graduated from Brown University with a degree in American civilization. Then she got her start on the coffeehouse circuit around Washington, DC.

Her first album, 1987's folky *Hometown Girl*, won critical acclaim but got little airplay. It wasn't until 1989's *State of the Heart* that Carpenter began to make her mark on country radio, with hits like the flirty "How Do?," the aching "Never Had It So Good," and the quietly regretful "Quittin' Time."

Even in those early years, Carpenter displayed an independent streak. At the 1990 Country Music Association awards, the then-thirty-two-year-old singer was invited to perform on the broadcast. But instead of singing one of her hits, she opted for a cleverly cutting song she'd been playing at her live shows: "You Don't Know Me (I'm the Opening Act)." With biting wit, the song called out a superstar "hat act" who had made opening for him on tour such an unpleasant experience that she felt compelled to write about it.

> *I don't have a hit on the Billboard charts*
> *I don't have a limousine that stretches three blocks*
> *Ready to take me from door to door*
> *Just like that jackass I'm opening for.*
> *He doesn't know me...*
> *I'm his opening act.*

It was a daring move for someone so new to the business—even without naming the song's egotistical star by name. But the audience's initial gasps quickly turned to cheers. The performance stole the show that night, winning the Nashville newcomer a standing ovation from the industry crowd. "It was a special opportunity and I did it," she would later recall. "I'll always remember that night. Michael Campbell, Ricky Van Shelton's manager at the time, was there during soundcheck and he was the last person I saw before I went onstage. Right before I went out, I heard him say 'That was a nice career you had going there, Carpenter!' When the audience stood and applauded, I was just flabbergasted."

Far from killing her career, the moment ignited it. Her third studio album, *Shooting Straight in the Dark*, became a critical and commercial success, launching four Top 20 country singles: "You Win Again," "Right Now," "Going Out Tonight," and the Cajun-tinged "Down at the Twist and Shout." By 1992, Carpenter was picking up the first of two CMA Female Vocalist of the Year awards and the first of five Grammys.

Radio embraced her as well. Her fourth album, *Come On, Come On*, became the biggest of her career, selling more than 3 million copies and spawning seven Top 20 singles. The album was full of irresistible hooks and poetic imagery. She was a lottery winner choosing between alt-country icons in "I Feel Lucky": "Dwight Yoakam's in the corner, trying to catch my eye / Lyle Lovett's right beside me with his hand upon my thigh." And she was a clear-eyed optimist daring the world to take its best shot in "I Take My Chances":

> *I've crossed lines of words and wire*
> *And both have cut me deep*
> *I've been frozen out and I've been on fire*
> *And the tears are mine to weep*
> *But I can cry until I laugh*
> *Or laugh until I cry*
> *So cut the deck right in half*
> *I'll play from either side*
> *I take my chances*

But the song that best epitomized Carpenter's unflinching worldview was "He Thinks He'll Keep Her," a feminist anthem inspired by a 1970s Geritol commercial where a husband compliments his wife's homemaking accomplishments before concluding, "I think I'll keep her." The lyrics depict a woman trapped in a stable but loveless marriage, caught between societal expectations and a need for self-fulfillment and independence.

> *She does the carpool, she P.T.A.'s*
> *Doctors and dentists, she drives all day*
> *When she was twenty-nine she delivered number three*
> *And every Christmas card showed a perfect family*
> *Everything runs right on time*
> *Years of practice and design*
> *Spit and polish till it shines*
> *He thinks he'll keep her*
> *Everything is so benign*
> *The safest place you'll ever find*
> *God forbid you change your mind*
> *He thinks he'll keep her*

In another era of country music, the woman might have stood by her man. But Carpenter's heroines never settled. Even when the cost of freedom is a job "in the typing pool at minimum wage."

Carpenter was never really a mainstream country artist, but by 1994, she had become a major Nashville star. And "Shut Up and Kiss Me," the first single from her fifth studio album, *Stones in the Road*, continued her commercial appeal, becoming the singer's first No. 1 single.

> *Oh, baby, when I feel this feeling*
> *It's like genuine voodoo hits me*
> *It's been too long since somebody whispered . . .*
> *Shut up and kiss me.*

The album also hit No. 1 on the charts, and won Carpenter two

Grammys in 1995—for Best Country Album and Best Country Female Vocal Performance.

But it seemed a turning point as well. Outside of the singles, "Shut Up and Kiss Me" and "Tender When I Want to Be," the album was quiet and introspective, a return to the singer-songwriter's folkier roots. Carpenter had grown older, along with all the twenty- and thirtysomething women she had given voice to. She married in 2002. Divorced in 2010. Life changed. Music changed. The world changed.

Her 2004 album, *Between Here and Gone*, included the haunting September 11 tribute "Grand Central Station," about an ironworker covered in "holy dust" escorting home the souls of the lost. I was on a train coming into Manhattan when those planes hit the World Trade Center. I watched the smoke pouring out of the buildings into that clear blue sky and, for weeks after they fell, stared each morning at the gray cloud that hovered over lower Manhattan. And in those dark days afterward, my heart shattered every time I walked past those makeshift memorials, where the faces of the missing stared out from walls papered with flyers. The onetime poet of the single woman had taken on heartbreak on a grander scale.

Eventually, Carpenter steered her career away from country, finding a home in folk and Americana and bringing her voice to songs about politics and social issues. Similarly, my own career was growing and expanding, my world enlarging with responsibilities and other interests.

Occasionally I will catch one of her early hits playing on a nineties country station, and I have to smile, remembering the women we both were back then—and how far we both have come.

Carpenter was never just the voice of the single woman. She was the voice of every woman who ever found herself at the corner of love and heartbreak and made a choice, not knowing yet what the future might hold. I'd been at that corner, made my choice, and taken my chances. I waited. I worked. I built a career, and kept thinking about what the future might hold for my personal life. "I never learned nothing from playing it safe," Carpenter once sang. Nor had I.

Twenty-six years later I am still living in New York, charting my own course, and, as an editor, pursuing the work that I love. There are still plenty of celebrity interviews and fabulous parties—along with more serious stories that remind me of why I got into journalism in the first place. The days are often long, the deadlines crazy. But when I pour myself into a car after another late-night magazine close, I know I'm doing what I was meant to do.

Carpenter's message was always simple: Be true to yourself and the world will fall into place. Sure, there may be days—or even years—of doubt, but hang on to your dreams. For dreams are the things that light our way.

And somehow, along the way, the rest of my life fell into place as well. In 2011, I met the man I had been looking for all along. One who shares my dreams and passions, and treasures the strong and independent woman I've become. We married in 2014, and at the wedding, we danced to Carpenter's 1996 cover of John Lennon's "Grow Old With Me."

> *Grow old along with me*
> *The best is yet to be...*

The best *was* yet to be. For all of us.

ell

PATTY LOVELESS

Beyond What You Know

WENDY PEARL

T he color scheme was cinder block and dust. Rose Al's was a local dive on the outskirts of the last remaining cow town in South Florida, and I was killing time between an afternoon monsoon and a city commission meeting.

The bar was long and pocked with chips and cigarette burns. I was perched on a stool—the sturdy kind, with chrome legs and a round vinyl seat that swiveled. With straight posture, legs crossed at the ankle, I was chatting up the bartender, a redhead with a wicked sense of humor. I was wearing a floral Laura Ashley dress in peony and mint with puffed sleeves and a ridiculous bow. No one was going to mistake me for a regular.

The usual clientele was a mix of bikers—mostly good, and some menacing—and the occasional cowboy from the surrounding dairy farms. In a few cases, the cowboys rode horses because they were waiting out a suspended license, thanks to a DUI or other misfortune. In the parking lot there was a cross tie for the ponies, pea gravel for the bikes. And occasionally one of the horses would use the handlebars of one of the Harleys as a salt lick.

To a stupidly ambitious reporter from the *Miami Herald*, it was editorial gold.

On this particular occasion, the bar was nearly empty. It was just me and a biker a few stools down. He was hunched over the bar with his arms crossed over a vanishing glass of Jack. I'd heard stories about him. He was in the Vietnam War and had a melon ball–sized crater in his forehead for his service. He was a little crazy. People—even the ones with bravado—gave him a lot of space.

Between us on the bar was a white plastic shopping bag. I'd heard about the bag, too. He used it to carry around a pair of breast prosthetics. I was avoiding eye contact.

"Hey, you. Hey, you, Blondie!" he said with a growl.

If I didn't answer, maybe he would forget me and move on to something else. But no such luck. There was literally nothing else to move on to.

"BLONDIE!" he barked.

I looked over, trying to appear tough. Sizing up how much trouble I could get myself into.

The bag was open. The gooey, pink breasts were on the bar.

"Do you want to touch my boobs?" he asked, like a dare.

I'm not known for the snappy retort, but I had one this time: "No thank you. I have two of my own."

"HA!" One syllable that sounded like gunfire: quick and ear-piercing. "I like you, Blondie. I'm gonna do you a favor."

I'd been on the receiving end of people doing me favors before. Mostly desperate sources with an angle to exploit. It was one of those words that set off my journalist alarm bells.

But caution never got in the way of curiosity, and I had an afternoon to kill; besides, I wanted to see where this would go. Ironically, the salty taunt and my plain naïve curiosity ended up changing my life.

"You see that jukebox over there?" he asked, nodding over his shoulder to the boxy neon machine with rows of typewritten names and song titles. "Play anything by Patty Loveless."

I asked myself just how this was doing *me* a favor when I was the one paying the tab, but I found enough quarters swirling around with the gum wrappers at the bottom of my purse to play "I'm That Kind of Girl."

I ain't the woman in red
I ain't the girl next door
But if somewhere in the middle's what you're looking for
I'm that kind of girl.

Hooked, I had to see if my reaction was a fluke. I punched in the number for "On Down the Line."

Doin' the best I can
Just trying to make a stand
Laughin' and cryin'
Living and dying on down the line.

I had never connected with a singer or a lyric in such an immediate and personal way. I was genuinely enthralled. The bartender and my biker Svengali seemed immune to my reaction, carrying on a new conversation while I stared at the jukebox, slack-jawed. I was hearing my life played out in neon and grit, sawdust and sass, like I had never heard it before.

Imagine a reporter, someone who tells other people's stories for a living, hearing *her* story, *her* life, *her* heartache. It didn't even seem possible, but there it was. I'd found meaning in the words and music of a coal miner's daughter from Pikeville, Kentucky.

It was the beginning of a very fulfilling, though admittedly one-sided, relationship that would sustain me for two decades, through marriage, motherhood, and a move to Nashville, where I would eventually work with my muse and watch her win CMA Female Vocalist of the Year.

In my experience, there are two types of reporters—good diggers and good writers. I fell solidly in the first group, with a relentless drive to learn as much as I could from as many sources as I could muster. I turned that laser focus on Patty.

Her story was nothing like mine—she is, after all, a first cousin to country royalty: Loretta Lynn and Crystal Gayle. But I connected on a cellular level with her authentic delivery, her rich honey-and-whiskey voice, and the way I *felt* when I heard her sing. She epitomized girl power before anyone knew about kinderwhores (on the punk side) or thought of tomatoes as being anything more than something you put on a salad.

I wanted to talk to her about boys. I wanted to talk to her about men. I wanted to take her out for a beer. I wanted to know how you cram that much living into a handful of verses and a chorus, and come out breathless and stronger and WISER.

I dug deeper.

Do you know how you sometimes discover something and you have the warped impression that you are the only person in the universe who "gets" it? That was me. I was wrong.

Patty Loveless was already a star when I found her on that jukebox. She was a member of the revered Grand Ole Opry (1988); she had captured the attention of the music industry innovator Tony Brown; she had already cut major records with songs by Steve Earle, Matraca Berg, Lyle Lovett, Kostas, Lone Justice, and Jim Lauderdale; and she was already on her second marriage—secret for a decent while—this time to her producer and creative equal, Emory Gordy Jr.

What I discovered was that the pain in her voice, the honesty in her delivery, her very vulnerability were forged on a path to Nashville that included hard lessons, personal sacrifice, and redemption. If I didn't, like Patty, have a perfect last name to scrawl in neon or Appalachian authenticity, I did have some of the same feelings driving me on a path I didn't know was ultimately going to take me to the very same place.

As a twentysomething too-serious-about-my-work reporter, I was searching for something—and I didn't know what. But under the façade of "I'm okay"—even when I wasn't—was a landscape shaped by my own parallel truth. I'd put in my time with stepdads and different schools, patching together an education and trying to figure out how to craft a career rather than just earn a living, without a clear road map—just a white-knuckle determination.

————

She was born Patty Lee Ramey on January 4, 1957. The family moved several times, following work in the coal mines. Eventually her father, John Ramey, would die of black lung disease, in 1979. To this day she remains committed to helping victims of lung disease.

She was fourteen, in 1971, when she made her first trip to Nashville. Her brother, Roger, was working with Porter Wagoner and eventually convinced his boss to give his kid sister a listen. Wagoner knew talent when he heard it. After all, he had taken Dolly Parton under his rhinestone-bedazzled wing.

Wagoner gave Patty a job opening for him during her summer breaks from high school. What she learned on the road influenced her art and shaped her as an artist in many ways—from developing a tireless work ethic to learning how to bring a room to its feet.

The Wilburn Brothers took notice and offered her a publishing deal, which gave her an additional outlet for her strong point of view as a songwriter. Her "voice" as a writer was unfiltered, raw, gutsy—and Nashville's finest tunesmiths were listening.

Graduating high school in 1975, she quickly found love with a drummer named Terry Lovelace. She took his name, which she would eventually change to Loveless because of local pronunciation.

Young love is rarely easy love. Sometimes the name you find ends up fitting you better than a custom-cut Manuel suit. In Patty's case, no matter how the girl waiting tables in a rundown diner alongside her mother-in-law tried, the fairy tale ran dry.

Patty and Terry had moved back to Lovelace's home in North Carolina, where he played any bar or hall with a sound system. In dry counties, he played private clubs or after-hours bars across county lines. When he realized there was more money to take home when his wife was in the band, he drafted Patty to sing as well as sling hash.

The kinds of places they were playing have the toughest audiences. The people who are there to forget, with the help of the whiskey, can get lost in the music, but mostly they are merely lost—and so was Patty, for almost a decade. Playing clubs with bullet holes in the walls, shouting over crummy sound systems, trying to find peace in a piecemeal world of delusion and false grandiosity, she was losing weight and losing ground.

Finally, her daddy came to get her. In 1985 she returned to Nashville, where a new generation of singers was emerging. With Emmylou Harris as the queen of the moment, Randy Travis and Ricky Skaggs suggested that Patty's bluegrass pedigree and soulful delivery might find a natural fit in the gritty, less-orchestrated sound of the neotraditionalist movement. She was home.

Not that it was easy to get noticed. Her brother knocked on every door, left mountains of messages. He finally trapped Tony Brown, the MCA wunderkind, A&R man, and producer, in his office—and promised to never bother him again if he'd listen to his sister "sing one song." Brown, the piano-playing gospel refugee, agreed. To him, three minutes of torture to shed this hillbilly nuisance seemed a fair price to pay.

Brown was stunned by the mountain authenticity and raw, gutsy pain of "The Sounds of Loneliness," a haunted song Patty had written at fourteen—and long her daddy's favorite, one he'd make her play and sing over and over. Staggered, Brown went from annoyed to enraptured; Patty was signed to a recording contract at the same label that had ushered in the then-burgeoning careers of Reba McEntire and George Strait, as well as soon-to-be critics' darlings Steve Earle, Lyle Lovett, and Nanci Griffith. It was only a singles deal—and Jimmy Bowen, the label head, said he couldn't stand to hear her sing behind closed doors—but Patty didn't care: she had a record deal.

But, in life as in her songs, heartache followed. She and Terry divorced in 1986.

She found her voice with Brown and a fellow Emmylou Harris Hot Band/Elvis Presley vet by the name of Emory Gordy Jr. The pair knew how to extract both emotion and strength from Patty's performances, matching her with progressive but hard country songs for a sound as eclectic and clever as it was traditional and sturdy. "Timber, I'm Fallin' in Love," from her second album, *Honky Tonk Angel*, took a play on words, shot it through with electric emotion, and added a decidedly mountain twang to her wild tone. It was a hit on country radio.

The magic between the members of the creative team reached beyond the music itself: Patty married Gordy in 1989. If no one knew—at least initially—about their wedding, their creative merger flourished. A string of singles ensued, including Lone Justice's "Toss Us Away," Steve Earle's "Blue Side of Town," Kostas's "On Down the Line," Matraca Berg's "I'm That Kind of Girl," the mandolin-driven "Hurt Me Bad (in a Real Good Way)," "Jealous Bone," and Lucinda Williams's first-ever cut, "The Night's Too Long."

But there's a big difference between having hits and really mattering, being in the game and being in contention. Though Patty Loveless was rocking my world, capturing my frustrations and feelings, she wanted to get her shot at Best Female Vocalist, to make albums that weren't compromised by a strain of mainstream country that felt watered-down and somehow not soulful enough.

Not that I knew any of this; after my introduction to her music, like so many people, I listened to the radio and bought the occasional album. I didn't know and I didn't need to know, nor did it occur to me to want to know. Patty Loveless made music that gave me a spark, an extra push or burst of energy when I needed it. The rest—well, I was just one more fan in the bleachers.

This, though, is where I come into the story. Only I didn't realize it at the time.

I had spent eight years at the *Miami Herald*. The work was good, and I loved it. Discovering and telling stories was my stock-in-trade—and I had found a kindred spirit in Patty Loveless. I connected to her as a storyteller. I connected to her as a woman. I connected to her as a late-twentysomething who was technically an adult but still frantically trying to figure things out. Heck, I connected to her as a girl who couldn't quite figure out dating and falling in love. She was singing my life in a way that no one had before.

It's not that I didn't *listen* to music; south Florida had a vibrant music scene, especially in the winter months, that covered the spectrum of sound and inspiration (and that included the soon-to-be-Grammy-winning Mavericks, on their way to becoming an international sensation). But this was different—not the fun of hearing hits or howling along with my friends, but, for the first time in my life, *feeling* music in my core. Not just a beat I could dance to, Patty's songs were my personal soundtrack, a witness to all I was living and learning. It was surprising and thrilling. And for the first time in my life, I was listening to Miami's country powerhouse radio station KISS-FM.

Patty Loveless's songs hit my life at an interesting time for reporters. It was the beginning of the nineties. The Knight Ridder executives with the offices overlooking Biscayne Bay were visionary. Way ahead of the curve in seeing what the advent of the Internet would do to daily papers, they developed an online newspaper before most people knew what online meant. For us reporters who were on a deadline, it raised questions about what was coming. Newspapers couldn't die, could they?

The *Miami News* had already folded, and there was a glut of really good reporters looking for work or desperately holding onto the jobs they already had. I could feel the weight of the glass ceiling pressing down; I knew I could cover city meetings or write reviews of fried chicken franchises for the next thirty years—or I could move on.

What would Patty do?

Crazy as it sounds to ask that question, here was a woman who'd done bold things, crazy things, and somehow survived. More than survived—made incredible music out of all she'd faced down. Asking myself that question, there was only one thing to do: I moved on.

There was the possibility of a job in Nashville with Sony Music. It was entry-level, and my existing salary would be cut in half, but to me it seemed like the Emerald City without the sleep-inducing poppies. I would be the coordinator in their PR department. I would manage interview schedules for the artists on the Epic and Columbia rosters, fill out endless streams of FedEx envelopes for music mailings, and write press materials that were grammatically correct (or close). On paper, it might've seemed too basic for a reporter who'd helped cover the outbreak of the Gulf War in our city. But that was paper, and this was real life. To me, it represented the thrill of a new adventure and the promise of something somehow greater.

I had no idea that at the same time that I was driving a U-Haul from Hollywood, Florida, to Nashville with the windows down, hair blowing wild, to take a job at Sony Music, Patty Loveless was planning a move from MCA to the very same label—the one where I would be licking envelopes and stocking shelves with CDs.

Her reasons were sincere. MCA's roster was packed with talented women—Reba, Wynonna, Trisha Yearwood, Kelly Willis—and there are limits to how many singles any label promotion team can push up a chart, let alone slots for the awards that many use to measure artistic achievement and momentum around an artist. Epic Nashville needed a powerhouse female, and Patty Loveless was the real deal, with her great song sense and a voice that was agony, exultancy, and everything in between.

I've noticed a trend with Patty Loveless. Just when there is something good in her life, the door opens wide for something bad. It happened again in 1992. On the brink of releasing her debut Epic album, *Only What I Feel*, she was diagnosed with an enlarged blood vessel. The only solution to the dire prognosis: surgery. Surgery on the very vocal chords that had brought her this far.

Everyone was devastated. People were whispering about, but no one would dare say out loud, what everyone was thinking: would she sing again? And if she did, would she sound the same? Would she still be Patty? It was the pain and triumph, as well as the desire, courage, and fun, in her strong muscular tenor that made her songs stand out for so many. More than how she moved columns of air around, it was the way her heart bled through on every single note.

She had the surgery on October 21. What followed was doctor-imposed silence, with whiteboards and gestures standing in as ways of communicating with Emory. There was time to kill while the label waited to see if its poster girl would reclaim her torn-from-the-holler voice. And yes, cruel people joked that "Sony Nashville bought itself a lame horse."

On January 4, 1993, Loveless was back in the studio, cutting the vocal for "Blame It on Your Heart." It would be the debut single on the new label, with a tongue-twister chorus destined to get people talking: "Blame it on your lying, cheating, cold dead-beating, two-timing and double dealing, mean mistreating, loving heart . . ."

Suddenly, she had *the* song, and any naysayers were silenced later that spring when Patty stepped onstage at the Ryman Auditorium—the Grand Ole Opry stage—and made her triumphant return. It was the very same institution where she had once sat backstage with Dolly Parton, who, while applying her makeup, told the wide-eyed, barely-teenage girl what singing and stardom required. Now the auditorium opened its arms to the grown woman with so much on the line. It was a safe place, hallowed ground, and symbolically, it meant coming home.

The timbre was there. The soul intact. The voice pristine—maybe even richer. People marveled, because the headstrong girl had grown into the kind of singer that could cause *Time* to marvel, writing about her "plangent voice" and proclaiming that she "gives us the truth, and she serves it up raw."

Standing in the wings, watching, I was speechless. I thought I was brave: leaving my mother, my job, my city where I knew every dive bar and place to get good Cuban coffee. Here was a woman who'd fought and found a foothold, run off and married, been brought back from a rough place she never spoke of, been given a long shot at MCA Nashville and been stymied by the number of women sharing the roster, made a dangerous move from the hottest label to one needing a heroine—and on the verge of "breaking through," had been told she might never sing again.

And here she was. Exultant. The moxie! Or maybe just the mountain heart.

A string of hits, gold and platinum records, Grammy nominations, and CMA Awards followed. If she'd gambled again and again, stubborn to the core—not willing to settle for anything less than music she believed in—she fought for the songs she felt in her heart. And what songs they were.

"How Can I Help You Say Good-Bye" followed a mother's love through the passages of her daughter's life, from moving away from a best friend to a divorce not wanted and, ultimately, to the mother's own death, while Gretchen Peters's "You Don't Even Know Who I Am" painted the dissolution of a marriage with such tortured images and wide-open grief, without ever blaming, that it stopped people in their tracks.

It wasn't *all* agony and moan, though. Matraca Berg's "You Can Feel Bad (If It Makes You Feel Better)" put the notion of her suffering all in the former lover's mind. Even the whimsy of "I Try to Think About Elvis"—a romp through images to distract her from obsessing about her new love—offered a wink that suggested the "suffering" was all in good fun.

She knew desire, in a way that was honest and real. Her CMA Vocal Event Award–winning duet with George Jones, "You Don't Seem to Miss Me," offered a last spark of want to a lifelong lover who was distracted or losing interest.

In 1995, *When Fallen Angels Fly* became only the second album by a woman to win the CMA's Album of the Year. Named for Billy Joe Shaver's song of redemption and rebirth, it offered a sense of hope to all who were worn down by life. Patty Loveless didn't gussy up reality into three-minute bits of positive uptempo froth—though she was capable of that sort of pluck.

In reality, when Patty went deep, America paid attention. With her dignity fought for and won, she showed people how to navigate their life disappointments and tough breaks—and she did it with so much emotion, she suggested the things you were feeling showed how much you cared.

Following your heart is harder than it looks. I know: I packed up a U-Haul and drove north to a place more southern than any-place I'd ever lived, to take a job I had no real background in. I left a man I loved behind. I went to a company—unbeknownst to me—beleaguered by politics and nonperformance. Along the way, I fell in love with music in a way I didn't know was possible.

I left Sony Music in 1994 to take a job at a boutique label with an eclectic roster and the maverick producer responsible for Randy Travis's career, Kyle Lehning. I got to work with Emmy-lou Harris—and the Harris/Dolly Parton/Linda Ronstadt trio—the iconic Texas songwriter Guy Clark, a young cancer survivor named Kevin Sharp who had a No. 1 hit with "Nobody Knows," and the wildly talented Patsy Cline–evoking Mandy Barnett.

Along the way, I never told Patty she was partially respon-sible for bringing me to Nashville. I never told her that her you-deserve-better mindset helped me hold out for the man I would eventually marry—who was the man I'd loved in Florida, and who eventually followed me to Tennessee—and still love two decades later. And I never told her she was my inspiration for raising a daughter who had pluck and verve as core values.

Looking back, maybe I should have. I had opportunities, but I'd seen so many other fans with trials of their own fill her per-sonal tinderbox with emotional matchsticks. I felt too guilty to add more. So I silently watched her career evolve, loved the incredible music she was making, and wished for her success, for all the things she had—unknowingly—given me.

That's the thing about Patty Loveless: she gives so much, and she doesn't realize it. By inspiring through music, she lets you believe in yourself—even when you're not sure you can.

I was watching again in 1996 when she won CMA Female Vocalist of the Year on the same stage where she made her comeback after surgery. Her husband was in the hospital, fight-ing for his life with severe pancreatitis, and he had insisted she go to the show. He knew that from the time she was a little girl listening to the Opry every Saturday night on WSM-AM—coming through a radio propped in her family's window and facing Nashville, as her mom washed the kitchen floor—winning the CMA Female Vocalist had been her greatest dream.

It was magical. And once again Patty was a harbinger of what was to come in my own future. I didn't know it at the time, but the pull of those awards would lead me to another major pivot in my life. Eventually I would take a job at the Country Music Association, where I would head the communications department and help advance the genre and the artists who make music all around the world.

Now I have been to London, taken the CMA Awards to Manhattan, watched my life—and my peers' lives—be populated with children, the passing of loved ones, the triumphs of careers, and, yes, disappointments, along the way. And with all of it, it seemed, there were songs.

I've been at CMA for seventeen years and have seen that many trophies handed out for Female Vocalist of the Year, but none of them meant as much as that one in 1996, when my musical muse stood on the stage that had so much meaning for her. Accepting this accolade from the industry that recognized her talent and determination, it was clear that she brought to this rapidly growing industry an authenticity and an honesty about who she was and what made the music matter to her—and she received a standing ovation.

Nothing has topped it since, and nothing ever will.

Like Patty Loveless, I never knew that my way was paved. I had no reason to imagine a life like the one I live now. I was a suburban kid in South Florida, doing all the things you'd expect. I was a reporter, chasing stories and looking for the heart beneath the facts. I was a young woman, not completely sure who I was but yearning for so much more. And, like so many girls who get their messaging from movies and magazines, I wondered how I could ever be more.

I didn't know. I didn't have to. I just needed a handful of quarters and the right kind of jukebox. Looking back now, it's hard to believe. But that's the thing about taking the time to pause and reflect, to sort it out and listen to the music. When you write it all down, some things become apparent. It's not what you plan, it's what hits you in the heart.

I have a war-weary biker vet to thank for the favor.

$\backsim\!\!\mathcal{elle}$

SHANIA TWAIN

———

But the Little Girls Understand

EMILY YAHR

In eighth grade, I had a social studies teacher who was tall and imposing, with a bold mustache. He wasn't easily won over. As a kid who was always eager to please my parents and teachers, I really, really wanted to impress him.

So when he offered my class the opportunity to participate in an essay contest, I jumped at the chance. What better way to show off just how dedicated I was than to do an extra assignment—*that wouldn't even count toward my grade*? I don't recall the exact topic, though the gist of the assignment was to write about a famous person you admired. Easy, I thought.

I turned in the essay a few days later and don't remember much about what happened next. I certainly didn't win the contest, so I didn't give it much more thought. But I'll never forget the expression of surprise, mild contempt, and amusement when my teacher saw the name of the person I chose to write about: Shania Twain.

Trust me, I have a lot of questions for my teenage self. Why, out of all the historical figures and pop culture icons I could have chosen, did I choose Shania Twain? Granted, it was the Shania heyday: it was the fall of 1999, and she was in the midst of becoming one of the most influential female country artists of all time, two years after the debut of her massive, ten-times-platinum album *Come On Over*, which would go on to be the most successful country album ever. Still, I didn't know any of that.

Why did I want to write about a country singer?

That question has loomed large in my life for the last seventeen years. Throughout high school, college on the East Coast, and my time as an entertainment reporter in Washington, DC, I constantly see my teacher's confused expression in my mind's eye when I tell people I love country music. "Why?" they ask, incredulous. Then the follow-up: "Where are you from?" When I answer "Ohio," they assume I must have grown up on a farm. When I tell them I was raised in the suburbs of Cleveland, they're confused all over again.

It's a hard concept to explain. Country music is an ingrained part of my identity. My fascination with the genre leads me to look at the impact it has on people and its significance in our culture. The fact that it's the most popular type of music in America says so much about us as a nation. Today I write about these questions for my job as a reporter for the *Washington Post*. But sometimes, even all these years later, I wonder where this passion of mine comes from.

I recently dug up my middle school essay to get some answers. Maybe, just maybe, it all started with Shania.

––––––

The document, miraculously still floating around on a CD-ROM in my childhood home, is titled "More Than Just a Voice." It begins with the following passage, verbatim:

Nowadays, everyone is always telling teens to go for their dreams. "Nothing can stop you! You are in charge of your own life! Your life is an open book with pages for you to write on!" And after awhile, they become some words strung together, not actual phrases with meaning. Year after year, teens head's are crammed with positive encouragement, that truthfully have no real effect. As a teenager myself in the almost new millennium, I myself admit I have only half listened when adults tell me those things.

Then all of a sudden, someone brought those words to life for me. Just one person. It wasn't my mom or dad, or even one of my teachers. They have done a fine job telling me that up until now, but one person made me sit up and believe it. And that person was a singer. I have no contact with her personally. But that doesn't matter. This one person brought across the message "never give up." Her name is Shania Twain.

That's a lot of passion. How did Twain inspire me? Read on:

Her road to becoming a singer wasn't easy. It was shocking actually, to learn how much she had to suffer to reach her dream.

We complain about how early we have to get up for school. Really? Well, how about getting up at one in the morning being dragged to various clubs to sing? Not really against your will . . . but knowing that you were nearly supporting your family of seven with the money you get paid? That is Shania Twain.

Going beyond my passive-aggressive swipe at my 6:30 a.m. wakeup call for school, I further explained Twain's other challenges: she had to press "pause" on her singing career in her early twenties to sing in a resort so she could support her siblings, after their parents were killed in a car crash in 1987. Considering that I didn't have easy access to the Internet, I'm not sure how I gathered this information, but that tragic story is true.

Throughout the essay, I contrasted regular teenage drudgery (chores, homework, too many after-school activities) with the hurdles that Twain had to overcome to launch her career, which started when Mercury Nashville signed her in the early 1990s.

I also wrote about how Twain didn't have time for a childhood—she had to help support her family by performing concerts at a very young age.

Analyzing the words now, I see that I was clearly feeling insecure and a little silly about my own complaints: as I learned more about the world, I realized other people had it *much* harder than I did. As a teenager, it often seems like the world is going to fall apart if things don't go exactly your way. But I knew I should be grateful for everything I had.

Twain's rough upbringing obviously struck another chord with me: that, to be successful, you couldn't make excuses. A repeated theme in country music, it's one that still hits home. Though I couldn't articulate it at the time, it was inspirational to see such a powerful woman achieve her dreams when she went through so much heartache. My essay concluded:

> I will always admire the woman who put everything before her career. Who never gave up no matter how bad it was. Who's songs tell the basics of life. Who everyone should strive to be like. Who is more than just a voice. Shania Twain.

While that spelling and punctuation haunt me, the "[whose] songs tell the basics of life" quote offers an important clue about why I connected so much with Twain.

I've wanted to be a writer for as long as I can remember. At age seven, I created the "Yahr Gazette." It had a comics section and an editorial page where, in second grade, I wrote a scathing op-ed when my parents informed me we were moving from Kentucky to Cleveland. I always had notebook pages filled with scribbled poems and stories. In high school, I decided to pursue journalism, a career that, I hoped, would enable me to write every day.

I suspect I started to relate to country music because of the storytelling, and the fact that many singers write their own songs. In middle school, I didn't know that Twain and her then-husband/producer, "Mutt" Lange, wrote *every* track on *Come*

On Over. I just knew that they were my favorite songs; not only were they fun, they related to all the things I was going through at the time.

The dreamy "You're Still the One" reflected how I felt about my middle-school boyfriend, and how smug I would be when we inevitably got married, even though my friends thought we were doomed. "From This Moment On," which my high school choir performed at a concert, would clearly be our wedding song. (We broke up in the ninth grade.)

Twain's supremely confident attitude informed her music. Shy and introverted growing up, I loved songs with swagger—when I belted them out with friends, it gave me a boost of confidence. "Man! I Feel Like a Woman" reminded me that, despite the awkward teenage years, glorious times awaited me as an adult who could "go totally crazy."

Even "That Don't Impress Me Much" had a place in my teenage life, as a helpful guide from someone older and wiser. I quoted the lyrics to my best friend when we discussed a guy who clearly had a crush on her, and who kept bragging about how well he did on his math test. We would sing these oh-so-relevant lyrics over and over: *"So you're a rocket scientist? That don't impress me much . . ."*

Eventually, my Shania fandom waned as I discovered other artists. But whenever I heard a Twain song, especially that guitar riff from "Man! I Feel Like a Woman," I was transported to that time between my childhood and adult years, when I was trying to figure out who I was, when I found inspiration and comfort in the songs created by a bold, confident woman.

———

In the 1990s, when female singers like Faith Hill, Reba, the Dixie Chicks, and Twain ruled the country charts, I took the place of women in country music for granted. Now, I frequently find myself writing about—and marveling at—the difficulties female country artists face in breaking through in the traditionally male-dominated genre.

Shania Twain burst on the scene with empowerment anthems like "Any Man of Mine," in which she confidently addresses her needs in a partner, and "If You're Not in It for Love (I'm Outta Here!)," in which she dismisses a man who's only interested in shallow hookups as he doles out lame pickup lines. Songs like the self-esteem-enhancing, feminine-embracing "Man! I Feel Like a Woman" still fuel think pieces today, with headlines such as the Odyssey Online's "Shania Twain: The Underrated Feminist Queen."

Though Twain, now fifty-one, hasn't released an album since 2002, she's still a force. With a two-year residency at Caesar's Palace in Las Vegas, she celebrated the career she built. But the high-energy entertainer isn't just inspiring nostalgia, she still wins awards—including CMT's 2016 Artist of a Lifetime. In 2015 she went on what was billed as her final headlining tour, even though she says that doesn't mean she's retired. Indeed, rumor has it that she might just be rehearsing again for some new shows, as the music in her blood still needs to be played.

In the summer of 2015, I finally had a chance to see her in concert. It was hard to know what to expect after all those years of waiting and wondering—but, from the fireworks and sparklers, to Twain flying around the arena on a mechanical bull, it was certainly a spectacle.

Watching the crowd carefully, I saw how the audience members of all ages, mostly adult women but also younger girls, reacted to the songs. They were remarkably similiar to each other as they got lost in the music. Whether dancing to the up-tempo hits or swaying along to the slower tunes, they were all consumed by the songs that had been so much a part of their lives.

At one point in the show, Twain sat down and talked to the audience about her life, and about a song she called a "cheerleading mantra." Relating to us like friends, she explained she wrote the up-tempo "Today Is Your Day" during a "particularly crappy time in my life," which one could only assume was when her ex-husband left her for her best friend, in 2010. The 2011 single must have worked as more than a cheerleading mantra: Twain found solace and understanding with, and then eventually married, her best friend's ex-husband. After the tabloid field day, she grew a beautiful life in the scorched earth.

Twain didn't elaborate onstage that night. She didn't have to. She just played the song, to wild cheers from the crowd. But as with all country songs, knowing there was a story behind the words made it so much more powerful.

I had gone to the concert to write a story for work, and as I often do when I'm covering big events, I tried to imagine what my fourteen-year-old self would think. If I had known that one day I would be writing about country music as my job, I'm not sure I would have believed it.

I may never really understand why Shania Twain struck such a chord with me at such a young age, but she certainly fueled my passion for country music; my belief in the power of connecting to songs through stories started way back then. It's a connection that now drives my life and my career.

And even though my social studies teacher was thoroughly unimpressed by my choice of essay topic, I remain grateful that I wrote that paper. Grateful that I trusted my own heart and choices and wrote about someone *who's songs* hit me as deeply today—albeit in different ways—as they did when I was young. Reading my essay now shows me how many parallels remain between my fourteen-year-old self and the woman I am today, still trying to figure out the world around me and using music to help me do it.

ALISON KRAUSS

Draw Your Own Map

AUBRIE SELLERS

W hen I was five years old, I heard a voice that swirled with sweet familiarity: a voice that felt honest to an introverted child of musicians who was beginning to discern between the real and the fake. *"Baby, now that I've found you / I won't let you go / I built my world around you."* Alison Krauss sounded like someone I knew and something I had never heard at the same time.

Growing up with a dad who played with Ricky Skaggs and a mom who vocally juggled sugar and twang, I knew bluegrass and I knew female country voices. Alison was both of these, and all her own. Her voice is as timeless as her records. It transcends genres as so few can, because it's so real, in the way that only singing with your actual unaffected voice can be. You get lost for a second when you hear her, not able to distinguish what era it is and not able to tell if everyone else has already discovered this or if you are the lone person in the world listening.

Of course, I had no idea that Alison was already a Grammy winner, and had been playing music since she was the same age I was when I heard her for the first time. I only knew what I felt when I heard her, and that feeling belonged in my world: Running around backstage at the Opry listening to my dad,

Ricky, and the Whites pluck and tune their instruments while I tried to follow the scent of popcorn to its source. Hearing my mom sing classic country songs around the house that she grew up listening to on my grandfather's radio show. Sitting in my uncle's green Dodge truck and listening to my eight-year-old cousin sing harmony with the songs on the stereo. Music was more than a hobby and more than a profession for the people I was surrounded by: it was ingrained in us.

My dad and uncle grew up on a bus, homeschooled by my grandmother, singing gospel music at churches, and perfecting the art form of family singing. I grew up the same way: on the run, independent, mostly spending time around people much older than me, not fazed by our alternative lifestyle because I didn't know any different.

Alison started young, too. She was born in Decatur, Illinois, in 1971. It only took five years for her to pick up the violin, and to turn it into a bluegrass fiddle shortly after that. She started young, like everyone I knew, and grew into music as she grew into life. She could have plateaued after winning contest after contest, but her talent only expanded and evolved over the years. Putting the time in helped her develop her chops, but so much of what makes Alison magnetic is something that cannot be taught: it's an essence that no one else in the world has, and that she was both born with and grew into over the years, as you can hear in her voice unfolding throughout her recordings.

I devoured movies from an early age, loved acting as a form of expression, and, considering my affinity for music, loved the marriage of both things. So it's not a surprise that the second wave of Alison Krauss in my life hit hard with the arrival of the soundtrack for the Coen brothers masterpiece *O Brother, Where Art Thou?* Alison's voice drifting along with those of Emmylou Harris and Gillian Welch, and floating over the congregation in "Down to the River to Pray," lent so much to the film, both rooting it and giving it the wings it needed to soar. Bluegrass lovers and those not familiar with bluegrass alike were overwhelmed by the raw, real soul the soundtrack granted the movie, which provided the perfect opportunity for Alison to shine to an even wider audience.

Honest voices move people and transcend art. Alison's career is laudable because she has never strayed from her core, and has been able to branch out into different projects without compromising those components that make her who she is. It's an encouraging story for young women who are unsure whether being themselves is the best option in a world where so much fraud—masquerading as "authenticity"—exists in what we are exposed to every day.

On her debut album, Alison sounds unbuttoned, backed up by raw banjo and lively harmonies, unleashing years of feeling. Two years later on *Two Highways*—her first record officially featuring Union Station—you can already hear her vocal command tightening, rounding out her spirit with that ethereal quality that is so often the focus of any conversation surrounding her.

But she is so much more than that.

She is sweet and sharp at the same time. There is an intensity behind her gentle voice that pushes further than you expect. She's a musician and a singer who understands music beyond the immediate world of bluegrass that she grew up in. Her discipline is heard in the quality of her music, and it has brought her twenty-seven Grammy Awards. She earned a good chunk of these for a record that came into the world at the perfect time for me to latch on to it, a time when I was truly considering my own place in the world and music; it solidified her spot on my list of all-time favorite artists.

There I was, a sixteen-year-old girl in my all-white shabby-chic bedroom, more concerned with procrastinating until the weekend when my friends were out of school than doing anything constructive. The familiar distant noise of someone rustling around downstairs in the kitchen was vibrating through the house, and the October air was drifting in through the windows from the small oasis of our west Nashville backyard. I had a freshly burned distraction in my hand, and I was thinking I would listen to this unexpected record once before forcing myself to attack the huge pile of dirty clothes in my closet. What would one more hour hurt? I popped the CD into my unremarkable but glossy supermarket stereo; what came out glued me to the floor for several listens. My laundry didn't get done that night.

Raising Sand took a well-established rock legend, Robert Plant, and a record-setting bluegrass songstress/musician, Alison Krauss, and combined their worlds into something completely fresh. At the time I was coming into my own, barely able to drive a car, and it collided with my evolving sense of self and growing awareness of how vast music can be. Having grown up on Alison, and having recently started devouring Led Zeppelin records, I encountered this: a masterpiece from an unlikely pair that was so clear and so right, and that landed at the perfect moment for where I was in my life. Hitting play and hearing "Rich Woman" come out of the speakers, I was immediately aware of Alison's willingness to expand and experiment. The record also fluidly demonstrated that her knowledge of music reached far beyond mountain standards and fiddle tunes.

She and Robert made harmonies magical again, in an entirely different way from the Alison already familiar to the world. Every single song on the album—from the raw honesty of "Killing the Blues," to the haunting melody of "Trampled Rose," to the raucous energy of "Gone Gone Gone (Done Moved On)"— spoke to me in a way nothing else quite had before. Like so much of her previous work, this record attacked with subtlety, and seemed to shift the whole world around you as you listened to it—and after.

My world did move, again. Like it had when I first heard Buddy and Julie Miller fuse dirty guitars and raw emotions, or when Loretta Lynn employed Jack White as her duet partner and whimsical producer. All of these far-flung musical elements that I loved—from grunge guitars to California steel—were running together like a band of perfect misfits, fleeing expectations and making no apologies. *Raising Sand* gave me the permission I needed to tread new ground and to believe that I could take these spare parts that I picked up and loved and create a new whole. Alison showed on *Raising Sand* that you could draw your own map, from start to finish.

Most of my life I appreciated my musical upbringing, but as a girl surrounded by musicians, coming into my own, I needed another outlet that belonged to nobody but me. I needed somewhere to escape to, where I could express all the observations of people's characters, both big and small, that I had made while growing up in an uncommon way.

For many years, acting allowed me to do that. I loved movies. I enjoyed dissecting all the little tics, reactions, and feelings that make a person and re-forming them into unique characters of my own. In an attempt to plant myself in another garden, to make art where I was in my own world, I went to California and studied at the Lee Strasberg Theatre & Film Institute. It allowed me to take all those feelings, all those observations, and twist them into expression. I engaged in a deep study of how bodies hold emotions, the way people react to each other, and I loved it. I loved everything about how creativity manifests there.

Something else was bubbling under the surface, though. I always felt it, as if it was waiting for the right time to come up. Every time I heard an album like *Raising Sand*, or an unfamiliar blazing guitar solo, whatever it was moved a little closer to the surface. When I picked up my guitar and started to write, it emerged fully. A lifetime of perceptions and melodies helped me begin to shape songs, and I met players and writers like Adam Wright, who got where I was coming from and were excited to try something divergent. The creative freedom that came from being fully in control of a project and going at it independently was new and intoxicating for me. Because of bold records like Alison's, I was able to trust my instincts, find people who understood, and keep pushing forward even when they didn't.

The major impact of *Raising Sand* was musical, but it may also have uncovered an understated truth that is important for any female musician aspiring to be independent and innovative. Being fearless, original, and authentic pays off. Alison did it on this record, and so many times before. She alternated between solo records and albums with Union Station. She turned pop songs and country classics alike into bluegrass anthems and did it all so effortlessly, you forgot the songs weren't hers to begin with.

As a young musician trying to find my path and learning to trust my instincts, that was all I needed to know. When music is something you live and breathe, you can only hold your breath for so long. I couldn't outrun my genes, and no matter how much I resisted following in the footsteps of my family, there was always a record inside waiting to be made. And I didn't have to sound like my parents, regardless of our vocal kinship.

I didn't need permission. I could sing with a tender twang over thrashing drums if I wanted to. I could unite dreamy steel with braying electric guitar. I could call out trivial magazines, cookie-cutter chicks, and cheap men alike and connect with other people who hate those things, too: people who grew up on country and who embrace tradition while rejecting the conventional. Hell, if there's no club to belong to, make your own. Thanks to *Raising Sand*, and all the other great records and artists I grew up on, my own brand of country—garage country—was born.

People will always put dauntless musical choices through the wringer, but in the end, there's a space for them—a space that wasn't there before, opening the world wider for others to connect and invent. For every person who is scared of something different, there are two people excited to find a space for what is distinct. I could say that artists like Alison Krauss break boundaries by simply being themselves, but it's only half true, because there is no other artist like Alison Krauss. She stands on her own. That's how a little girl from Illinois grew up and put a *big* mark on the world. And in some ways, an even bigger mark on me.

TERRI CLARK

———

Better Things to Do

AMY ELIZABETH McCARTHY

W here I come from, there's really only one way to be a girl. You quickly learn that, as a young woman in East Texas, it's your responsibility to be blonde, get married, and bear children. You're supposed to sit quietly and laugh at the Wrangler-wearing, wannabe cowboys' jokes in the hopes that one will be willing to put a ring on your pretty little finger and whisk you off to a happy life of cooking dinner and raising babies.

None of that ever really made sense to me, an awkward fat girl with a butch haircut and a mouth too big for her own good. I knew that I was never going to be one of *those girls*, the ones who actually fit into the Rocky Mountain jeans and set the boys' hearts aflutter. As such, I started to distance myself from that identity in the most deliberate of ways—I dressed weird, I said too much, and I listened to a whole lot of Terri Clark.

In the late 1990s, Faith Hill and Martina McBride ruled the country airwaves. It was a new era for country music, one in which women were outselling and outperforming men with regularity for the first time, but that ascendancy was paired with a whole lot of high expectations for these artists. They had to be larger than life, their voices as big as their stage presences and their long mops of hair. As much as I liked to sing along with them on the radio, I knew that Faith and Martina really weren't my kind of girls, either.

A blue-collar Canadian brunette with a deep timbre and a penchant for wearing tank tops and singing about NASCAR racing, Terri Clark fit in with this crop of new country queens about as well as I fit in with the homecoming court. It never really occurred to me that Terri Clark probably also felt a lot like an outsider when she first arrived in Nashville. She played the city's honky-tonks at a time when traditional country just wasn't selling records. It was an unlikely stardom: Terri Clark was brash and tomboyish, and she didn't look a whole lot like any of the rest of the girls or sound like them. But she's the woman who taught me how to be a real, authentic country girl.

It always struck me as strange that Terri Clark recorded so many love songs. When I first heard the chorus of "Poor, Poor Pitiful Me," I assumed that it was about someone like me, stuck in a small town dying of boredom and the sort of unfulfilled wanderlust that only a deeply dramatic nine-year-old can feel. But no, a closer listen would reveal that my woe-is-me track was really about a bunch of stupid men chasing a girl who was too fast (in many respects) for them.

I was deeply disappointed. *How could someone so unique and interesting and independent be so enraptured with what boys thought about her?* But then the speakers of my Aiwa bookshelf boombox were filled, immediately after, with "I've Got Better Things to Do," and with that laundry list of mundane tasks—all of which were more important than crying over a boy—Terri Clark had completely redeemed herself as my badass queen of the backwoods. And then she was gone.

By the time high school rolled around, I had cultivated the most intricate of defense mechanisms against what I hated most about living in my small, podunk town, populated with shit-kicking, dip-spitting hicks and the women who bend over backwards to make them happy. I worked tirelessly to cover my East Texas/Louisiana–twinged accent with something that sounded a little more sophisticated. I dyed my naturally blonde hair an inky black. I wore chain-store pseudopunk clothes. I had decided that if these people—my neighbors and classmates and all those damn boys—wouldn't have me, I'd make damn sure that they really, really didn't want me.

In 2003, Clark released "I Just Wanna Be Mad," and in that song, I truly heard myself represented on the radio for the first time. Anger in a young woman isn't exactly something that's cultivated in the South. You're supposed to sit still and look pretty, but I'd never done a particularly great job of hiding my angst; even my fiery, independent mama wished I'd go along to get along a little bit better.

I think I'm right, I think you're wrong
I'll probably come around before long
Please don't make me smile
I just wanna be mad for a while

On the face of it, Terri Clark songs don't really seem all that revelatory. Maybe they don't include the intricate metaphors of a George Jones tune or Loretta Lynn's country-fried backstory, but that's actually kind of perfect for an adolescent girl trying to figure out who she really is. At that point in my life, I hadn't experienced any real heartbreak other than the melodramatic kind that comes with pining for a boy who doesn't—or won't ever—want you.

But it was endlessly easy to identify with Terri Clark: she was accessible, the kind of girl you think you can actually grow up to be. Lord knows, even then I was already too fat and surly to be raised up in the image of Faith Hill. Clark gave me permission to be angry, to refuse to accept the place at the table that was set for me. I probably didn't realize then how much that song influences who I am as a person today.

Still, I spent most of college pretending that I really liked Bjork and bizarre noise music, which is what you do when you're a young adult who fancies herself a real intellectual. But in Lubbock, Texas, you're never too far away from good country music. The home of Natalie Maines and a place where countless Texas Country stars (think Pat Green and Cooder Graw) cut their teeth, Lubbock is a place where you almost can't avoid hitting the honky-tonk for some live music on the weekends. Hell, there isn't anything else to do.

Eventually, a pair of red cowboy boots found their way back into my closet for the first time since grade school, and the tunes of Johnny Cash, Loretta Lynn, George Jones, and Tammy Wynette started creeping back onto my iPod. I discovered the incredible world of female singers in folk and bluegrass, genres which had until this point been reserved for guys like Neil Young and Ralph Stanley, at least in my mind. And there was always, always a Terri Clark playlist in the mix.

As it does, life happened, and music somehow found its way onto the back burner. I worked shitty jobs, listened to whatever was on the radio, and paid the bills. At twenty-four, I found myself laid off from my full-time job and stupidly decided to take a whack at writing for a living. I'd always enjoyed it so much as a kid, filling countless notebooks with fantastical short stories and the highly philosophical ramblings of someone who listened to a little too much Bob Dylan. Why not try to make a little money doing it?

Then, of course, came the question of what the hell to write about. A twenty-four-year-old isn't an expert on anything, except maybe finding cheap booze and avoiding bill collectors. I saw an ad at my local alt-weekly for music writers, and I figured I'd throw my hat into the ring. I quickly realized that everyone in the world wants to be a music writer, because it's the most deceptively cool job on the planet.

But not everyone wants to be a *country* music writer. It's much cooler, and as a woman you get so much more "cred" in this male-dominated industry, if you're into the weird new electronica act from Sweden. But I knew I'd never be able to even approximate an interest in listening to that shit. I had always loved country music, despite a long absence from listening;

I thought I knew it well enough; and I figured that I could bullshit my way along until I figured it all out.

At the same time, I immersed myself in country music's incredible history. I listened to all the Bob Wills and Ray Price and Johnny Cash in the world, slowly building a foundation of knowledge that felt like my childhood rushing back in bursts of colorful nostalgia. I taught myself all about the incredible women who had broken down barriers just to be on the same playing field as the boys. But I constantly went back to the women of the 1990s, the chanteuses who soundtracked my rides to school and church. And I especially kept coming back to Terri Clark.

And that has everything to do with the fact that Terri Clark was a trailblazer in her own right. Faith and Shania and Martina may have made it commonplace for women to sit at the top of the *Billboard* charts, but there was never anyone as gritty, as raw, or as authentic as Terri Clark. She was a female Dwight Yoakam, pairing traditional instrumentation with a raw honesty that was fresh, aggressive, and sometimes uncomfortable. Her bold, brash guitars and uniquely gritty sound undoubtedly paved the way for women like Gretchen Wilson, Miranda Lambert, and Angaleena Presley to have a place in this genre.

I remember listening a lot to Clark's 2012 album, *Classic*, which never even made it to the *Billboard* Country Albums chart. It may not have had a whole lot of mainstream appeal or even been all that memorable, but listening to Clark reimagine some of country's most iconic songs, like "It Wasn't God Who Made Honky Tonk Angels" and "Don't Come Home A-Drinkin' . . . ," was revelatory for me. The real watershed moment came when I heard Clark's slow-burning cover of "Delta Dawn." Featuring smoky harmonies from Tanya Tucker herself, the song made me realize that my own country identity was still here and always had been. It had just been buried in a place that I wasn't ready to dig up yet.

Now, ten years later, you're much more likely to find me clacking the heels of my gold-flecked cowboy boots on the floor of a honky-tonk than at some obnoxious, experimental DIY house show. My country bona fides are no longer up for debate, whether or not I fit the identity—which still persists—of what a country girl is supposed to look like. Now I have the confidence to happily sneer back at the snotty broads who glare at my dark, often goth-y lipstick and my flamboyant (yet nerdy) rhinestone-encrusted glasses.

And when I look back at Terri Clark through this lens, I see a woman who didn't quite get to where she wanted to go. Her place in country music history may well be overshadowed by those artists who found a great deal more commercial success than she ever did. But whether or not most people realize it, what Terri Clark did for women who don't quite fit the mold in country music—and in real life—can't be ignored.

I feel like I'm proof of that. I've firmly staked my place as a ballsy and bona fide country girl in too many ways to count, and that has everything to do with Terri Clark. I know now that my voice is powerful and worthy of being heard, whether or not it is as polished or pretty as the voices of those other girls. We're both outsiders, Terri and I. Both not quite what the world wants in a woman. But I know now that women like us, the ones who recognize the power of our emotions and being completely, sometimes painfully, honest with ourselves, are the ones who get to live a life that is wholly authentic.

TAYLOR SWIFT

Dancing on Her Own

ELYSA GARDNER

My first meaningful encounter with Taylor Swift's songs took place about a year after my daughter was born. It was the fall of 2008, and I was covering pop music and theater for *USA Today*; Swift, then a few months shy of her nineteenth birthday, was about to release her second album, *Fearless*. For the second time in a pretty short span, I had no idea what I was in for.

Swift was already a big-enough deal by then that critics were required to listen to the album in the confines of a record company office, as opposed to getting a stream or (more likely at that time) a disc delivered to them. Her self-titled debut album, featuring songs she had written as a high school freshman, had topped *Billboard*'s country and pop charts two years earlier. Still, she wasn't really on my radar; I'd heard singles such as "Tim McGraw," "Teardrops on My Guitar," and "Our Song" mostly in passing, and while charmed by their unfussy sweetness, and impressed by her youth, I hadn't been compelled to listen more closely. My colleague in Nashville was set to interview her, though, which meant the review fell to me. (In those days, newspapers still had the resources to acknowledge potential conflicts posed by having one writer both profile and review an artist for a given project.)

I did some homework before hearing *Fearless* for the first time, which would at least mitigate the shock that came with giving Swift—who had matured quite a bit between the ages of sixteen and eighteen, as girls are prone to do—a fairer chance. I learned she had grown up listening to a variety of music but had set her sights early on Nashville, presumably because storytelling and songcraft were higher priorities in country music than in pop at the time. Swift valued such things, and wrote songs that could stand alone, propelled by a single guitar or piano if necessary. Songs that pulled you in and stuck with you, without congealing in your ears.

Sounds like an easy task if you've never tried it, but consider how many popular artists have managed it well enough to transcend genre boundaries, after starting so young, while also evolving and enduring as popular performers. It's a pretty short list. And if I didn't leave that office convinced I'd heard the next Carole King, I was blown away by how compelling this teenager's melodies and narratives were, and how clearly and confidently they reflected her own vision. As I wrote then:

> For the past decade, the term singer/songwriter has been liberally applied to hot young artists who rely on more experienced collaborators to hone their tunes, and to provide the savvy production that usually upstages the melody and lyrics anyway. But Swift cut her creative teeth in Nashville, where storytelling still matters; and for her sophomore album, *Fearless*, she wrote more than half the songs independently, and clearly had a big hand in the rest.
>
> You just can't fake the kind of innocence and wonder that ring through the glowing title track and the moonstruck single *Love Story*, or the guileless urgency and unmannered precociousness marking more bittersweet love songs such as *Fifteen* and *White Horse* . . . It's a pleasure to hear a gifted teenager who sounds like a gifted teenager, rather than a mouthpiece for a bunch of older pros' collective notion of adolescent yearning.

I'm sure the "innocence and wonder" held added resonance for me as a relatively new mom, just as Swift's subsequent music, and the growing pains it reflected, would resonate as my child grew and eventually discovered the songs herself. Swift's lack of pretense and attention to craft were also high on the list of virtues I'd come to cherish in my earliest years as a music lover, listening to the soaring scores of Rodgers and Hammerstein musicals and the exquisitely produced pop of Michael Jackson (with Quincy Jones) and ABBA.

As my tastes broadened, I remained wary of artists who seemed self-consciously transgressive, or who traded too heavily in angst. I had little patience with the reluctant rock stars bred by punk or, later, grunge, or indie acts that bemoaned the mindlessness of pop music. They reminded me of the goth kids who pierced their cheeks and dyed their hair purple so that they could get as much attention as the students they mocked—among them gals like Swift, who kept their eyes on the prize and didn't pretend not to care. Though hardly the overachiever Swift is, I could, as a former suburban high-school drama-club officer who never missed a curfew, relate to her unapologetic squareness; it was strangely exciting for me, in fact.

So was her genuine autonomy. By the early aughts, I'd noticed that a growing number of recording artists—male and female, many of them a lot older than Swift—were listing themselves as one of three or four or six writers on tracks that, indeed, were often less songs than they were vehicles for killer arrangements. There are financial incentives for this practice, of course. Credibility is an issue as well; since the advent of Bob Dylan and the Beatles, some critics and industry insiders have fostered the false notion that interpretive singing is a lesser art form.

But that's the subject of another essay. The point here is that Swift was, and is, a songwriter first. No appreciation of her music, or of all she has accomplished and endured while becoming one of the planet's best-selling artists and most prominent public figures, can be valid without accepting this—and understanding how it is necessarily complicated by her lack of a

Y chromosome. Many who caught sight of the ethereal beauty wandering through the video for "Tim McGraw" surely assumed she hadn't written the song, and not just because country singers generally face less pressure to be part of that process than their peers on the pop charts.

By the following year, when "Our Song," Swift's third single, made her the youngest performer to top *Billboard*'s Hot Country Songs chart with a song she had written alone, most folks knew better. Her backstory, that of a precocious Pennsylvania native who had studied acting and singing before her family moved to Nashville to accommodate her rising creative ambitions, was known to anyone paying attention, and it belied stereotypes applied to pretty blondes and girls singing about boyfriends. Indeed, the world didn't know it yet, but Swift was about to shake up the music industry by reclaiming the latter category, songs about young women in relationships—also Carole King's turf, decades before—for young women in relationships.

Swift did this without making gender a looming sociological concern. However her songs may take men to task, they seldom start from an assumed position of disadvantage; there's a sense that she hasn't spent much time pondering how being a woman might hold her back in life. Here, too, I've felt a certain kinship: like Swift, I'm lucky, having been raised in a comfortably middle-class home by parents who never pressed me to marry young or questioned my ability to work in a field that was, at the time I started in it, fairly male-dominated. I haven't been subject to harassment or abuse at work, or elsewhere; to the contrary, I think gender worked to my advantage in a profession (journalism generally, arts criticism specifically) in which leaders have been actively promoting diversity in recent decades.

I'm fully aware that many women don't share my good fortune, as is Swift, I'm sure. I also know that were I by some crazy twist of fate a famous songwriter who drew primarily on personal experience rather than on my political views, listeners might not be inclined to label me a feminist. But no less popular a champion of women's equality than Lena Dunham defended

Swift in a 2014 *Rolling Stone* article: "She runs her own company, she's creating music that connects to other women instead of creating a sexual persona for the male gaze, and no one is in control of her. If that's not feminism, what is?"

The plight of "women in rock," as it was called in the eighties, when I was a teenager reading *Rolling Stone*—and again in the nineties, when I was a regular contributor—had, of course, been the subject of hand-wringing for decades before Swift emerged. As a novice reporter, I was repeatedly called on to ask female artists if they felt oppressed or underestimated or pigeonholed. (Most were polite enough not to point out that I was pigeonholing them myself by posing these questions.) Still, young women who mined their own experiences and imaginations became pop stars, inspired by the central role earlier female artists had played in the singer/songwriter movement. In Nashville, women who could both write and sing with maddening dexterity, like Gretchen Peters and Matraca Berg, saw their own profiles rise while crafting hits for other artists.

Music charts reflect cycles, though, and Swift arrived after something of a fallow period for women and for singer/songwriters in general. The bubblegum-pop resurgence that spawned Britney Spears and the Backstreet Boys in the late nineties had been followed in short order by *American Idol*, which reduced interpretive singing to vocal preening and brought back the retrogressive premise that singers are primarily vessels for producers, or "music experts," as the self-promoting suits who would get rich off the series (led, loudly, by Simon Cowell) sometimes called themselves. If *Idol* launched the careers of one of the new century's most formidable vocal talents in Kelly Clarkson, and one of its most durable stars in Carrie Underwood, neither has been able to entirely shake off the program that, like subsequent TV talent competitions, has treated contestants as malleable savants at best.

Before transitioning to Swift, we must first consider Beyoncé, who predated the other millennial icon on earth and on the charts, and who has sustained the same level of ubiquity. It was she who, even while using cowriters more liberally than Swift, reestablished the concept of the autonomous female pop star, the diva running her own game. The two women remain gracious foils, and not just because of race or musical style. (As high priestesses of pop and women on top, they share some influences, obviously.) Those who would emphasize the relative slightness of Swift's warm, delicate voice miss the point: As an entertainer and vocalist, Swift's greatest strength is not her indomitability but her relatability, along with the will to excel that enabled her to essentially learn to perform in the spotlight. There were bound to be some awkward moments along the way.

Which brings us to Swift's first crucible as a public figure—one that, incidentally, involved Beyoncé. Contrary to Kanye West's subsequent boasts, Swift was already a superstar when she appeared at the 2009 MTV Music Video Awards. *Fearless* had debuted at No. 1 on the *Billboard 200* chart; the album would collect Grammy Awards, in 2010, for both Best Country Album and Album of the Year, with "White Horse" earning additional trophies for Best Country Song and Best Female Country Vocal Performance.

It was another single from *Fearless*, "You Belong with Me"—a timeless capsule of teenage longing, wistful but ebullient—that earned Swift a VMA for Best Female Video and, thus, West's ire. The incident (in case you don't remember, or were living under a rock at the time) began with West storming the stage as a nineteen-year-old Swift was preparing to accept her Moon Man, and grabbing the microphone out of her hand (promising, comically, that he'd return it). The rapper then protested that Beyoncé, nominated in the same category for "Single Ladies (Put a Ring on It)," had delivered "one of the best videos of all time," before handing the mic back and running off, as Swift stood looking like a doe in the headlights.

Beyoncé managed a characteristically classy rescue later that evening: after "Single Ladies" was awarded Video of the Year, she called Swift on stage and offered the latter a chance to accept her own award, properly. The women, both dressed in bright red, hugged, and came out smelling like roses. As for West, President Obama surely spoke for most of the nation at that time when, in an unguarded moment, he called him a jackass.

But what's most disheartening about this episode, in retrospect, is that West's temper tantrum didn't carry anywhere near the vitriol that other "haters" have shown Swift in the years since—to put it in the parlance they, many of them women, would use. Too young, too thin, too cute, too calculated, they've charged, directly or implicitly. Too forthcoming, not forthcoming enough. Too much of a goody-goody, too much the opposite.

Such clucking about talented and/or good-looking and/or famous women is nothing new. But thanks to exponential advances in technology since Swift's arrival, now schadenfreude junkies need only push "send" to get an instant high. As a digital native, Swift has both wielded social media's mighty sword—championing new artists and promoting friendships and business alliances with equal avidity, as her more than 85 million followers on Twitter and 100 million on Instagram could attest—and felt its edge.

It can be hard, surely, to reconcile the prom queen with the lovesick girl who had to turn to her guitar to express her feelings. But Swift's protestations of humility, while striving for and securing prize after prize, hardly make her unique among high achievers, in any field. If millennials may be less inclined to take this into account, I'd propose that that's partly because of the unforgiving pop culture they've grown up in—a culture in which stars are resented as readily as they're worshipped, because fame is something we can all covet and feel we deserve. Whether your ticket to it is a perfectly constructed song or a sex tape that goes viral is considered, by some, to be of little consequence.

The proliferation of social sites catering to our basest impulses has hardly been the only factor in this sad shift. Professional media organizations, in a desperate scramble for relevance and profit, have in some cases become the haters' most devoted allies. "People don't want to hear pretentious artists talk about their craft," an editor told me a few years ago, perfectly summing up the snarky populism shaping a lot of today's "content," as it's now called. It's both the more mundane and the more salacious subjects, according to this philosophy—ticket sales, pregnancies, divorces, petty rivalries, sartorial scandals (and triumphs), disease, death—that hold the most interest for "media consumers," as we're now called.

Inevitably, other aspects of Swift's artistic and social life were scrutinized in these pieces: her alleged feuds, the various members of what the media calls her "squad"—high-profile friends, among them actresses and models, whom Swift is regularly spotted hanging out with—and, of course, her dating life, the subject of especially keen fascination and disapproval. Because, hey, none of us dated more than two or three guys in our twenties, right?

It's certainly fair game to consider Swift's relationships in listening to her music; since releasing her third album, *Speak Now*, in October 2010, she has pretty much invited us to do so. I still remember the raw shock of first hearing "Dear John," rumored to have been inspired by a romance with the substantially older John Mayer. "I lived in your chess game . . . Wonderin' which version of you I might get on the phone," Swift sang, resolving, "You'll add my name to your long list of traitors who don't understand." I don't know Mayer's side of the story, but listening to Swift's account was like watching something soft harden, knowing its constitution had been changed forever.

In fact, each of the songs on *Speak Now*—all of which Swift wrote independently—seemed intended for a particular person or group of people. "Back To December" was widely perceived as an apology to another ex, the actor Taylor Lautner, while speculation held that "Better Than Revenge" targeted an actress who lured then–teen idol Joe Jonas while he and Swift were dating. (Swift didn't name names, but by now, she didn't have to; fans and critics alike could go diving for dish online and just fill in the blanks as they liked.)

Swift had emerged as a confessional singer/songwriter just as the line between celebrity and artist was disappearing altogether, so that it was impossible to separate one aspect from the other. Lists have been compiled connecting each former flame to a song he inspired, though Swift has been skillfully vague about her subjects, responding to questions about her personal life with discretion and occasionally refuting rumors outright. "If you want some big revelation, since 2010 I have dated exactly two people," she told *Vanity Fair* in 2013. "And the fact that there are slide shows of a *dozen* guys that I either hugged on a red carpet or met for lunch or wrote a song with . . . it's just kind of ridiculous."

That prurient interest could work to Swift's advantage, though. The actor cast in "We Are Never Ever Getting Back Together," the lead single from her next blockbuster album, 2012's *Red*, bore a much-noted resemblance to Jake Gyllenhaal. In an interview with *New York*, Swift referred to "the guy the song is about" in her fashion, without either identifying him by name or insulting him. There was, to be sure, nothing demure about the song itself, a lithe, muscular piece with a singalong chorus, cowritten with the pop savants Max Martin and Shellback. Never mind the roots guitar jangling in back of the verses; this was pop candy at its toughest and tangiest, with a feminist bent perhaps made more digestible, though not diluted, by its sense of humor.

"Never Ever" was, incidentally, the first Swift song that got my daughter's attention; she was just turning five at the time, but I'm sure some of its exuberant defiance reached her. A few years later, I asked why the song appealed to her; being her mom's kid, she first replied, "The melody," but then elaborated: "She dumps a guy who's not being nice." To demonstrate, my daughter sang, "You go talk to your friends, talk to my friends, talk to me . . . ," smiling the whole time, showing how Swift, without losing her cool, let the dude know he'd no longer have her ear, or anything else of hers.

As my daughter approached her tween years, I came to

better appreciate the sense of independence and self-worth that Swift's songs can transmit on an almost subliminal level. If anything, Swift's ability to reach the very young has grown stronger as she has matured: *1989* offered songs that appeal to our capacity for self-actualization and sheer joy in the most basic ways, from the chart-topping "Shake It Off," with its exuberant prescription for stumping haters, to the wide-eyed wonder of "Welcome to New York," to the blithe "How You Get the Girl," in which Swift put a different spin on the "Never Ever" scenario, so that respect and forgiveness prevail.

Though *1989* would be marketed as Swift's first "official" pop album—and make her the first woman to win two Grammy Awards for album of the year—it was really *Red* that confirmed her place as a Top 40 artist first and foremost. Noted country producers such as Nathan Chapman, who had been with Swift since her debut, and Dann Huff also worked on the latter. But the songs—many penned by Swift on her own (among them the bittersweet title track), some collaborations with high-profile contributors, including Ed Sheeran and Dan Wilson—were, above all, showcases for a by-now-inescapable personality. In a YouTube chat, Swift said, "They're all pretty much about the kind of tumultuous, crazy, insane, intense, semitoxic relationships that I've experienced in the last two years."

Just as significantly, they emphasized Swift's adaptability as a singer over her technique. Having evolved into a global superstar at a time when production mattered at least as much as singing or songs, Swift crafted tunes that accommodated her assets; that were both substantive and accessible. Turning out a spare, stunning ballad such as "All Too Well" (co-written by Liz Rose), or a folky midtempo number like "Everything Has Changed" (the collaboration with Sheeran, who also sang on the track), Swift wielded her voice with wit and feeling, with the intuition of a natural musician and an authenticity affirmed by years of having her choices scrutinized and continuing to draw openly on them anyway.

However charmed her young life and career seemed, Swift

approached both strategically, and this is key, too: nothing seemed either inevitable or hugely surprising about her success. Consider, again, Beyoncé—also a master strategist and tireless worker, but one who has made it all look effortless. Or, conversely, Adele, with her working-class background and voluptuous figure, propelled by a huge voice and aching vulnerability laced with a saucy sense of humor. Or Rihanna, the muse that roared, a feral, regal presence with her finger fixed on the zeitgeist.

Swift is, her jaw-dropping achievements notwithstanding, less of an outsized presence than any of these artists. There's a sense that she's simply earned her perch in the pop stratosphere step by step, with a determination and discipline that might have served her well in any number of fields. If all artists have a need to be loved, Swift seems to have a need to be liked as well—something that most women who have aspired to success can relate to, perhaps too keenly. When asked to explain how her art and life intersect, her tendency to omit names but provide details suggests a woman struggling not to betray the composure and grace and strength that have defined her as an artist.

In 2014, Swift insisted to *Rolling Stone* that *1989* was "not as boy-centric of an album, because my life hasn't been boy-centric." She added, "I feel like watching my dating life has become a bit of a national pastime. And I'm just not comfortable providing that kind of entertainment anymore." In fact, Swift winked at this pastime in another crazily catchy hit single, "Blank Space," which like "Blood" had been co-written with Martin and Shellback. "Got a long list of ex-lovers / They'll tell you I'm insane," Swift sang, then underlined the joke: "Darling, I'm a nightmare dressed like a daydream."

That last line became a favorite for my daughter, who was seven when *1989* was released. The word "sassy" had become a staple of her vocabulary by then; it was used to reprimand her at times, but she had also gleaned that, under the right circumstances, a sense of assertiveness and humor could serve her quite well. Like many of her friends and classmates, she had been completely captivated by Swift; what girl could resist those scrumptious pop hooks, that bright-red lipstick, the mix of sweetness and attitude?

Many mothers received Swift with similar enthusiasm, after a period in pop music that had seen Miley Cyrus morph from tween idol to twerking enthusiast, and that produced hits such as 2014's "Fancy," in which Iggy Azalea boasted of being "in the fast lane" and "takin' all the liquor straight" while teasing and then rejecting a guy. Again, I noticed something of a generation gap: some younger women I spoke with (though not all) found artists like Azalea and the more imaginative Nicki Minaj funny and even empowering in how they reversed or sent up clichés embraced by hip-hop and rock's baddest boys. Comparisons have been made, obviously, to Madonna, whose provocations sent the parents of more than a few Generation Xers reeling.

But Madonna sang, primarily, about love. Flirtation was a means to that end, not a defense mechanism or a sign of acquiescence. Swift also brings that spirit to her music, albeit dressed very differently and with a few decades of progress to her benefit. The equality between men and women is a given for the younger star (if not for the wider world), and not just in matters of the heart. With her decision to temporarily withhold *1989* from Apple Music, and to write an open letter to its CEO, taking the company to task for not paying artists for music streamed during a free trial period—leading Apple to reverse that policy—Swift showed as much business acumen as any power broker who made national headlines that year, and more moral authority.

By 2016, Swift was appearing in ads for Apple Music, spreading the love, as is her wont, by lip-synching to tracks by other artists. The clips showed her at home, grappling with her treadmill, putting on makeup: just like us, as a certain popular magazine feature would label it—but of course nothing like us, in that Apple would not enlist many of us to goof around in front of a camera. (And were the company to do so, the featured musicians likely wouldn't get a fraction of the attention Swift provided.)

There are still stars, and artists, who rightfully enjoy such privileges. And who inspire us, whether we're middle-aged critics looking for affirmation that pop culture hasn't become a contradiction in terms, or nine-year-old girls, as my daughter is now, standing in front of the living room mirror, singing: "I never miss a beat / I'm lightning on my feet / And that's what they don't know . . . I'm dancing on my own." She will eventually know more about the frustration behind those lyrics, from "Shake It Off"—and, I hope, feel more of the exultation in them. For now, dancing on her own is enough.

KACEY MUSGRAVES

Follow Your Arrow

DACEY ORR

I t was the last song on *Same Trailer, Different Park* that hooked me. The easy strumming intro and quiet ambivalence made "It Is What It Is" a love song for someone who wasn't in love. It had a quality I came to love in a lot of Kacey Musgrave's music, in that it didn't require superlatives to get the point across. You didn't have to be in the midst of some great love to have another human take up space in your brain. You didn't have to be at rock bottom to be having a tough time. You didn't have to be in crisis or mid-epiphany to be worth writing about.

The lyric that struck me as the most original made me feel kind of callous, really: "Maybe I love you, maybe I'm just kind of bored." As a twenty-two-year-old with a footnote of a personal life, I knew that feeling. I had a guy I couldn't quite shake, but I never knew whether to call it love or a bad habit. That kind of uncertainty—and the extremes I bounced between—populated the other areas of my life, too. I was stumbling through my first year out of school and working as a music editor. It was the job I had always wanted, but as the youngest person in the room (even when that room included my own interns), I would enjoy brief moments of pride in my work followed by drawn-out periods of self-consciousness and mild panic that I was going to screw it up.

"It Is What It Is" and *Same Trailer* in general were an acknowledgment that the contradictions and the in-betweens I was experiencing could be worth writing about—poetic, even. "I Miss You" felt prescient in the moments in which I took stock of a career win or a milestone and still didn't feel quite whole. "Keep It to Yourself" took over every time I tried to rid myself of my own not-quite-relationship and fell right back in. I was "Blowin' Smoke" and I was "Stupid," too, but the more I clung to that record, the more I realized that maybe I wasn't alone in those things.

Writing about *Same Trailer* was my first stab at fusing my love for country music with my fledgling writing career, and my interview with Kacey Musgraves was only my second in-person interview ever. (My first one, with a rapper in Atlanta, began with him introducing himself as Sugar Dick, so it was hard to imagine things going much worse this time.) I met her backstage on the Kenny Chesney tour—a tour I'd spent my first summer out of college working on before settling down in my editorial job. Chesney was my big leap after college, and it was a gig most people didn't really expect for me. My relationship with country music had always been circumstantial, listening to the radio at a tailgate or being blasted by cover bands at a bar. But attending twenty-four country shows in three months will either make you crazy or make you fall in love with the whole spectacle, and I had decidedly fallen into the latter category. This was my first shot at explaining that love to my peers, and I was cripplingly anxious at the thought of my two music identities colliding.

"Come on in," I remember Kacey saying as she opened the tour bus door. "Sorry there's makeup everywhere. Can you believe it's just up to me to make my face not look so crazy?"

I've always loved the way she said that about the makeup. It was this immediate, self-deprecating admission that I really connected with. It was just like that question I'd been asking in one form or another for a year now: *Can you believe anyone trusts me to do this by myself?*

The ice was broken, and the interview went about as well as any interview could have gone for a nervous newbie. In the weeks and years that followed, I found myself following the business of country music a little closer, rooting for Kacey as she straddled music industry stratospheres that seemed to demand many different things from her all at once. I beamed every time a new critic or too-cool indie writer hailed her as country's down-home dose of the twenty-first century, and I took it personally when I felt she was dealt a bad hand. I remember one big Nashville DJ making a fuss to his fans about how she'd been during an interview, and thinking about it still makes me red in the face. Really?—you're rude now, if you're not chirpy and giggly? (If that was his idea of a rude interview, I can only assume he'd never been asked to call his subject Sugar Dick.) As someone who wasted a lot of time feeling too young and inexperienced to write with authority, watching the way *Same Trailer* resonated with others the way it resonated with me made me hopeful and confident. "Follow Your Arrow" didn't just make country a welcoming space for all kinds of people; it eliminated the need to be a particular *kind* of person at all. In Kacey's world, you could be a gunslinging Texan who supported gay marriage, a virgin who cracked up at crude jokes, or a country singer who revered tradition and got down to a twangy "No Scrubs" cover.

If *Same Trailer* was the record that let me know I didn't need to be everything to everyone, *Pageant Material* was the record that found me taking active control of who I would be and with whom. By the time that record was announced, I'd been at my editorial job for almost three years; country music had effectively gone from being my guilty pleasure to my glorified beat. I'd learned that being alone could make me feel refreshed and not rejected. I'd gone from feeling timid about publishing my work at all to actively seeking out criticism, pitching editors I didn't know on stories I wasn't sure I could write, and figuring it out as I went along. When Kacey debuted "Biscuits" and announced her new album, my pitch on an updated profile about her was met with a good-natured "duh" from the other editors at my site—a vote of confidence and, to me, a challenge to make it something meaningful.

I set up a time to interview Kacey backstage at Bonnaroo, the festival that had sealed me on landing a career in the music industry when I'd attended as an intern years earlier and the first place I'd seen Musgraves perform, in 2013. Even so, I went into the weekend a ball of nerves. I had just turned in my first print cover story, a feature for the *Village Voice* about a first-time (and now-defunct) country festival in New York. I'd been buried in edits on nights and weekends on top of my full-time job, trying to flesh out a piece that explained to New Yorkers how country music was booming, how some blowhard had said that women were tomatoes in the radio salad, and what those things might mean for music fans in general. For all of the confidence I had built over the last two years, my brain was a highlight reel of worst-case scenarios. I was traipsing around the enormous festival grounds with my laptop on my back, checking my e-mail furiously in case I needed to stop, drop, and edit. I was worried that my interview with Kacey would devolve into another anxiety-ridden item on a too-long to-do list that I needed to spread out over a dirty, bleary-eyed weekend on the farm.

But when I got to the stage and saw her rhinestone-studded set, the tightness in my chest dissipated. I don't recall the set list or what she started with, but when the easy notes to "High Time" rang out, I vividly remember this elated feeling—a mix of recognition, confidence, and preparedness set to steel guitar. *Pageant Material* wasn't even out yet, but I knew the record backwards and forwards. For once, I didn't feel like a fake. *Can you believe anyone trusts me to do this by myself?* This time, that question had an answer. *Of course.*

Being a midtwenties southerner who hadn't quite found a stereotype to settle into, I was thankful for the understated confidence of *Pageant Material* the way you are thankful for a stranger who tells you your teeth have lipstick on them or who lends you a tampon under the bathroom stall. Missing someone on the road, having a crazy family, falling short of expectations, or needing to chill the hell out—it's like every time I pulled out the album, *Pageant Material* recognized what I needed and served it up. This record wasn't the veiled middle finger to the Nashville establishment that critics were clamoring for, and it wasn't an overt appeal for airplay, either. And it didn't need to be. What I loved about *Pageant Material*, and about *Same Trailer* before it, was the same thing I loved about that initial greeting when I first tiptoed onto Kacey's tour bus: in them, I saw a reflection of bits of myself.

I still doubt my writing and get those anxious feelings, but when the tightness creeps into my chest I've learned to channel the kind of calm that washes over me when I listen to those songs. Looking for that glimmer of sameness with someone or something—not just in music but in people and professional situations and love and friendships—is the best way I've learned to quiet the anxiety and to be at peace with my own shortcomings and capabilities. Kacey has so many lyrics that speak to this point. "It is what it is." "I'll just do me, and honey, you can just do you." "Nobody's everybody's favorite, so you might as well just make it how you please." "I'd rather lose for what I am than win for what I ain't." The lyrics that push me to accept my own insecurities are the ones in which I hear a reflection of my own doubts—the ones that aren't so different from that initial question that calmed me down on the tour bus. "Can you believe it's just up to me?" *Can you believe anyone trusts me to do this by myself?*

RHIANNON GIDDENS

A Gift Past the Songs

CAROLINE RANDALL WILLIAMS

R hiannon Giddens has been a bright light ahead of me since I met her. About ten years ahead, to be specific. In the summer of 2007, she was thirty, I was two months shy of my twentieth birthday, and I had a summer internship with a company that makes soundtracks for movies.

The movie in question was Denzel Washington's *The Great Debaters*.

I landed in Shreveport in the early evening. The music team's unofficial headquarters was an inauspicious Comfort Suites. I took a Crown Vic taxi to the hotel, unpacked, and then found myself almost late for dinner.

My boss and his right-hand, Adam, had selected a Mexican restaurant. While we waited for a table, I met Alvin Youngblood Hart, Dom Flemons, Justin Robinson, the late, great Sharon Jones, and Rhiannon Giddens. I was in over my head. I was delighted and terrified.

I did not know that I should know who these people were. I knew that I wanted to anyway. There was an eminence to the group as a whole that was undeniable. But from the start, Rhiannon had this luminosity of spirit that made her my anchor throughout the days on the set.

I was overwhelmed. I was a young nineteen. I could barely drive and I'd never been in love. I'd just realized that maybe I wouldn't be a movie star. But I was watching Denzel Washington do his work from up close. It was a gift. It was magic.

The set pieces on which my five-day trip centered were the two juke-joint scenes, which featured all of the musicians. We filmed in the middle of the night, in a wooden shack in the Shreveport Bayou. I say Shreveport, but really, that juke scene set was right on the Louisiana-Texas border. I never quite knew which state I was in.

Late June in Shreveport, Louisiana, is not for the faint of heart. It is swampy, and the mosquitos are possessed of a ferocity I've known nowhere else in the world. But I thrilled at watching this group play their music. I had never seen or heard anyone quite like Rhiannon Giddens. She made music that was wild and fresh to me. She was making a life in art. She was modeling a way of being in the world that made sense to me. It is hard to say how rare a thing that was—and is—for a young black woman, ten years ago and still today.

Though it is the least substantive of her virtues, at least to a fan like me, it is the most obvious: Rhiannon Giddens is a beautiful woman. To me, at nineteen, she was like a Janie, walking back into town wearing those overalls, with her long locks down to *there*. She's the good hair and high cheekbones that tell stories of all of the places and people it takes and means to be colored, to come together to make a colored girl.

Her music tells that same story.

I needed the idea of her then. I need it even more now.

In my writer's heart, Rhiannon Giddens is the child of Shug Avery and Hank Williams—the light-skinned, high-yellow black girl with the Irish name and a sound so fresh and so old all at once that she speaks to me from every direction.

When we met in that summer of 2007, her family was new, her big-deal music career was still in that liminal space between a big dream and a big hit, and she was wearing pigtail braids and a beat-up flowered cotton dress in a Denzel Washington movie on the bayou.

There is a place for brown girls in the country world. There always has been. I grew up occupying some of that space—a child of the movement, if you will.

But Rhiannon Giddens was and is something else, for me and to me. Who dares to field holler *and* twang? Who dares to find a blues in bluegrass that deepens the love of both sounds? Who could do this but our girl? But this woman?

This is a woman who studied opera in a conservatory. This is a woman who is unafraid of the dichotomies inherent in embracing the full scope of southern musical influences. She can call a square dance. She makes her home in Ireland, a testament to the rich and ongoing ties that bind Gaelic sounds to those of Americana music. She called her first band Sankofa Strings. Sankofa is a Ghanaian word that demands exactly what Giddens does: it says, look to the past and bring it back.

Intersections or crossroads are, to me, the most American spaces. All modern American music is a hybrid. As it should and must be. Rhiannon Giddens is a hybrid, as she must and should be.

Just listen to her Grammy-nominated album *Tomorrow Is My Turn.* From "Waterboy," a field holler written by a Romanian immigrant, to the title track, penned by a French balladeer, to a jazzy, rhythmic reimagining of the Celtic classic "Black Is the Color of My True Love's Hair," she never shies away from her old-fashioned, idiosyncratic tastes. She takes us all deep into Diddy Wah Diddy with songs like the purely bluesed "Shake Sugaree," the bone-rattling spiritual "Round About the Mountain," and the sweet good word of "Up Above My Head." She lets herself be all things to herself. With "Don't Let It Trouble Your Mind," she covers Dolly Parton as if she's Bob Dylan's girlfriend who just can't let him have the last word after "Don't Think Twice, It's Alright."

It's a testament to my ignorance that I didn't know "She's Got You" was a Patsy Cline cover until after I had imagined

Rhiannon's musical birth mothers, but it also speaks to how inevitable and essential her music is, and how undeniable the necessity of her addition to the country music canon.

By some wonderful gift of grace and history, we are living in a world of black girl magic, a world of black first ladies, seats at tables, and *Lemonade* with an uppercase L. Rhiannon Giddens, with the way she is unabashedly herself—a black woman making music that defies limitations of genre, race, or even time—is a revelation.

There are so many of these liminal spaces in the world of music and the world of the South. The places where genre and color intersect. There are so many ways to be in between or on the edge of a thing, of a sound.

The Carolina Chocolate Drops literally and figuratively flavored the Appalachian sound. Watching them come together to make music helped me make sense of the southern spaces I occupied growing up, with Aretha Franklin playing on the stereo and Steve Earle sitting in the living room. Spaces where gutbucket country meets blues-blacked soul. Where light brown skin tells hard southern stories.

It almost seems as though Giddens takes everything good, anything she likes, from the American musical milieu—the bent blue notes, the grassy strings, the lament in the back of the throat that transcends borders of time or space. She takes these things and renders them, through her one new American country sound.

During that week working on *The Great Debaters*, I spent days on set chatting a bit, helping where I could, and watching Rhiannon make music with her band. I knew they were onto something. I surprised myself with how shy I was. She surprised me with the generosity of spirit that is the hallmark of how I remember her.

We would set up for the night shoots in the late evening, when the sun was gone but there was still an indigo in the sky. That is the best time to get eaten alive by the mosquitoes, and Rhiannon and I must have seemed some type of meal.

They'd given her a tiny trailer; to spare me from the mosquitoes, she shared it with me. I can't recall much by way of air conditioning—we fanned ourselves with our hands. We simmered. We chatted. The walls were white. The floors and the ceiling were white. The lights buzzed bright and glaring. Rhiannon and I looked at both of our high-yellow selves in the mirror. Her fiddle between us on the one thin bench for sitting. And she made me laugh. Talked to me like I was grown. Showed me what it could look like to be young and black and wild and country and brilliant and *about* something.

When she left to film, I would follow, and watch the shoot from a tarp spread over the wet, dark earth. I crept so close to the monitor that Denzel called me out, said, "I see you peeping, girl. Get over here." He put his headphones over my ears, and let me look, for real. I was hardly ready for this immersion. The sound of a real country blues, in a space faithfully crafted to look like spaces that no longer stand, transported me. And there was Rihannon in the fray, in the bayou, slapping her hands and head, singing and free.

I was taken outside of time then, and I am taken outside of time again, reflecting upon it now. This must be that sense of Sankofa she meant when she started. Here I am, nearly the age she was then, listening to her on repeat, hoping I do as right by my dreams as she did, and continues to do, by hers. Her music is a gift past the songs.

PATTY GRIFFIN

Remembering to Breathe

KIM RUEHL

F rom about 1995 until about 2004, I was hell-bent on the
notion that my purpose in life was writing songs. I wrote
hundreds of them: love songs, heartbreak songs, political songs, pop songs, country songs, show tunes, songs about
my pets, songs about life on the road. I was your standard-issue
American folksinger: ripped jeans, cigarettes, purple hair, and all.

I hit a rough patch around 2001, after moving to New York
City to see how far I could take it. I'd prepaid my summer sub-
let and my train ticket out there (on Amtrak's Empire Builder,
from Portland, Oregon, clear across the country), and I'd saved
enough money to carry me through the season. I arrived in Manhattan on June 3, moved into my West Harlem apartment, and
went to work on being a professional musician, whatever that
meant. Those three months were the first time in my life—and
the only time—when all I did was make music. I only knew one
subway route in New York: the one I'd ridden when my mother
and I visited NYU, which had been my dream school. So I took
it from my apartment to Washington Square Park every day. I
sat there and wrote and played, and played and wrote. I played
every open mic in the city until people started hiring me. My

first gig was at the Orange Bear in Tribeca. I think I made about eight dollars. I had arrived.

I played everywhere that would have me: the Sidewalk Café, the C-Note, Meow Mix, CBGB Gallery, B3, DTUT, Kenny's Castaways. I survived on cheese pizza and bodega coffee. But by the end of the summer, my money was running out and I needed to either find a job (and a new apartment!) or leave town. I landed at the Gap, World Trade Center, and moved into a beautiful second floor walkup in a brownstone in Bedford-Stuyvesant. I was on my way to work one morning when planes flew into the World Trade Center. Instead of folding denim and telling strangers they looked good in those jeans, I spent that morning first running for my life, then stranded in a café in the West Village (it was my then-girlfriend's first day of work there). By midafternoon, we were allowed to walk home over the Manhattan Bridge, with the skyline—a strong jaw with two missing teeth—burning behind us. It would be months before those fires went out.

Everything changed.

I spent another year in New York. Some days I smoked two packs of cigarettes—not good for a singer. I still played whenever and wherever I could, but the joy was gone. The only time I was interested in making music, or, really, doing anything, was when I was communing with my friends or at a vigil for all those lost in the WTC attacks. At night, I waffled between nightmare sleep and insomnia. Many nights, I took to wandering Manhattan at 1, 2, 3 a.m., totally wired. I'd sit by the river and write poems, sit in the park and watch the sun come up. I knew I needed to leave New York if I was going to get my self back. A new friend offered me her broken car if I could fix it, so I did. Then I booked three months of gigs between New York and Portland, and got the hell out of Dodge.

The car—a red 1974 Volkswagen Beetle named Lucy, with one orange fender—broke down in New Orleans, and that city sucked me in. It does that to people. I was sleep-deprived and loving life. I found a girlfriend, drank and ate a whole lot, explored every bit of the city, remembered how to celebrate and relax. But I was also neck-deep in posttraumatic stress disorder, living in a rough neighborhood with gangs and crackheads wandering through. It was the best of times, it was the worst of times. I tore free of the Crescent City's magnetic pull after nine months, and eventually found myself and my guitar on a Greyhound bus from Orlando to Seattle.

Seattle, with its hills and mountains and lakes and bay, was a wide-open, fresh start. All those giant swaying evergreens. There was so much fresh air there, and I desperately needed to breathe it. I knew, by then, that I needed to do some serious healing, and I even sort of knew that I was done chasing the dream of being a singer-songwriter, though it would take me another couple of years to truly move on. After all, I'd been making and studying music since I was five years old. It was the only thing I could conceivably refer to as "my skill set." If I wasn't going to chase the dream, what could I possibly do?

Of course, I met a girl.

Karen worked for Microsoft, but she also happened to be one of the most talented piano players I've ever met. What she lacked in technical prowess, she made up for with an impeccable ear and wildly creative melodic insight. She was the kind of person that can hear four bars of a song, then sit down and flesh out the rest of it while barely thinking.

We started dating, and then we started a band. We recruited a multi-instrumentalist named Dean and a cellist named Broer. Karen's keyboard managed, magically, to be both the melodic driver and rhythm section. It was an inspiring and maddening collaboration. She had no interest in being a full-time professional musician, and neither did anyone else in the band, except for me. It wasn't long before I had to face the music, as they say: I could bail on my girlfriend and Seattle and the band to pursue my songwriting career, or I could stay put and learn and become grounded in ways I had never before imagined. I chose the latter, and then I got a day job. After a few fits and starts, I wound up writing for a living.

Meanwhile, Karen's other band was called Skitterpup. The group, which also included two-time National Fiddling Champion Colt Tipton (they never failed to introduce him as such), mostly played bluegrass covers of their favorite songs, with the occasional original tune thrown in for good measure. They had three solid vocalists, who slayed when they lapsed into harmonies (their version of Dolly Parton, Emmylou Harris, and Linda Ronstadt's "The Pain of Loving You" was a favorite), and it was that vocally swollen approach to Patty Griffin's "Love Throw a Line"—along with Colt's always perfectly placed fiddle—that made me fall for the song, normally performed to about twenty people in a chai house in Seattle's University District neighborhood.

By then, I had begun to supplement my marketing and catalog copywriting job by contributing CD reviews to *West Coast Performer* magazine. The imperative of listening to music for at least part of my day—deeply listening, figuring out what worked and what didn't, then finding a way to explain it all—kept my songwriter brain functioning and proved a fun little challenge. It was a new way to consider music, to channel my knowledge and experience for something other than my own songwriting. It was inspiring. I started looking for more and better ways to do it.

One of the jobs I landed had me writing for a Web company called About.com, who put me in charge of their "folk music" topic. My editor was a friend of a friend, who knew about my songwriting career and encouraged me to start by profiling folksingers I loved. About.com was soon purchased by the *New York Times*, which raised its profile, and suddenly I was on record company mailing lists. People were sending me music every day, and my job was to listen to it, understand it, and form an opinion about it.

One of the albums I glommed onto quickly was Patty Griffin's *Children Running Through*. I'd heard her name but had never really heard her—unless you counted Skitterpup's bluegrass take on her song. But, because Karen and her band seemed to have a thing for Patty Griffin, I gave that disc some extra-open ears. It turned out to be stunning, exactly what I needed.

As I mentioned, I had spent the previous six years in the throes of PTSD—a state that places your nervous system perpetually in fight-or-flight mode. It reorients your ability to tell the difference between a safe space and an urgent threat, and everything I'd learned about it indicated there was no cure, only learning to live with it. But as I sat there and listened to Patty Griffin sing, "Stay on the ride / it's gonna take you somewhere," I felt the birds in my belly start to fly away. I could breathe again, deeply.

The disc begins with Griffin taking a breath, in fact, and then someone counts her in and she just *goes*. Vocals and a distant bassline, brushes on the snare. With distance between who I am now and who I was then, I now hear the song as a rumination on a lover—a relationship that just plain didn't work, and the song's narrator is the only one who sees it. She's moving on, with equal parts hope and regret, and yet . . . Back then it felt like a dedication to my future self from my present self. It's basically seven lines total, but it came to me like a promise for the future. "You'll Remember" reminded me that life unfolds, that there were more than a few days still ahead. That no matter how far I could see, the future was there, waiting.

There were other songs, of course. Emmylou Harris backs her up on "Trapeze"—a song that I took, perhaps because of the album's title, as following a child's imagination way far over the line. ("Just seventeen / already divorced.") I loved the way Griffin backed off and let Harris—who had the harmony, not the lead—move to the front. Their voices—powerful, strong, full of wind and water—swing past each other like the trapeze about which they're singing. Behind them, there's some barely-there guitar fingerpicking. Musically, it's an achievement: on paper, there's almost nothing happening, but the performance is everything. Even the twangy ring of the high E string at one point feels like the snap of a trapeze support. The way the singers build to the "hey hey" outro almost entirely on the strength of their hand-in-hand crescendo is just tremendous. But it was the line "Some people don't care if they live or they die / some people want to know what it feels like to fly" that really got me. Another tug back to the idea of taking chances, of trusting something, of trusting oneself.

Then comes the one-chord jangly mess of "Getting Ready." I spent a decade trying to get my guitar to *not* sound like that: like tap-dancing across a floor fashioned out of razor blades. It's all metal against metal—a nails-on-a-chalkboard tone. And yet here it was, working, wielded as the backdrop to an empowerment anthem. An epiphanic twist to a bad relationship saga. All these themes: change, trust, hope, determination. I'd forgotten these things even existed, and Griffin wrote songs—and sang them—in a way that reminded me.

But it was the one-two punch of "Heavenly Day" and "No Bad News" that, then and there, just stripped off all my dark clothes. "Got no trouble today," she sings, "with anyone." The space between the lyrics felt like the flap of a lone hawk in a blueberry sky. I hadn't been able to see past that one beautiful day and those two planes, but this song flipped a switch to where I could once again see a beautiful day as just that.

> No one at my shoulder bringing me fears
> No clouds up above me bringing me tears
> Got nothing to tell you, I've got nothing much to say
> only I'm glad to be here with you on this
> heavenly, heavenly, heavenly, heavenly, heavenly day

She climbs the mountain of those "heavenlies" until her voice is at the clifftop, and then it jumps—and soars, coming in for a soft, subtle landing on the song's final note. She slides into the tonic, and all the notes around it just dissolve, like dust kicked up. It's a healing song. It healed me. It heals me again and again, to this day, every time I hear it.

Griffin, who grew up in Maine, wrote the album after moving to Austin for love and then promptly losing it. She told NPR's

Steve Inskeep in 2007—the year *Children Running Through* was released—about how she learned to sing from her mother, who used to sing all the time when Griffin was little. "It's not the words she's singing; it's the feeling," Griffin noted, explaining how that same quality has seeped into her own music. And yet, while Griffin's voice carries with it a certain melancholy longing—her songs often sound like the first thoughts of morning or the last before sleep, those moments when we're most vulnerable and open—her voice would be an empty, gorgeous instrument without the words she writes for it.

They often come most strongly in couplets, simple and unguarded phrases such as in "Mary," from her 1998 release, *Flaming Red*. That song considers the mother of Christ from a feminist perspective, doing the work of motherhood, of being a wife. "While the angels are singing his praises in a blaze of glory / Mary stays behind and starts cleaning up the place." There's "Kite Song" (from 2004's *Impossible Dream*), where she sings, "In the middle of the night / the world turns with all its might." On 2002's *1000 Kisses*, she lands a heartbreaking narrative: "You could cry or die, or just make pies all day / I'm making pies."

With her 2014 release, *American Kid*, she dug into her family line and delivered the redemptive heartbreaker "Go Wherever You Want to Go," which she wrote for her father after he died. Among other couplets, there is this one: "Working like a dog's not what you're for now / you don't ever have to pay the bills no more." A child's love for her parent, the mourning of loss, and the incredible sadness and universal truths known deeply by the working class are wound together there. It's a folk song line if ever I heard one. It's the kind of line I tried my whole songwriting career to write, and she just drops it in the middle of a song, in a pile of comparable lines, like she grows these things in her garden and just collects them into bouquets.

These days I don't mourn my songwriting career anymore, because I know Patty Griffin is writing. She writes the songs I wish I could write, so I figure the world is covered in that regard.

A decade or more into my accidental career of writing about music instead of playing it, I sleep well most nights, thanks in no small part to the sense of home I get from my wife and my daughter, and the tall swaying pines in the Blue Ridge Mountains, where I live. There is plenty of fresh air here, after all, and no shortage of heavenly days.

Carter | Lil Hardin | Wanda Jackson | Hazel

Cash | Brenda Lee | Bobbie Gentry | Loretta Lynn

a | Emmylou Harris | Barbara Mandrell | Tanya T

| Linda Ronstadt | Rosanne Cash | The Judds | k.d.

ns | Mary Chapin Carpenter | Patty Loveless | Sha

Krauss | Terri Clark | Taylor Swift | Kacey Musgra

nnon Giddens | Patty Griffin | Maybelle Carter | L

Jackson | Hazel Dickens | June Carter Cash | Bren

entry | Loretta Lynn | Dolly Parton | Emmylou H

Mandrell | Tanya Tucker | Rita Coolidge | Linda

ne Cash | The Judds | k.d. lang | Lucinda William

n Carpenter | Patty Loveless | Shania Twain | Aliso

rk | Taylor Swift | Kacey Musgraves | Rhiannon Gi

Griffin | Maybelle Carter | Lil Hardin | Wanda

~ele~

THANK YOUS

———

Tbis book would not have come about without the bottom-less faith of American Music series coeditor David Menconi, who has been a cheerleader for my vision and my writing for years. When I told him I needed to postpone, again, the Emmylou Harris book I owe the series because this anthology needed to be written, he patiently sighed. Also, a massive thank you to acquiring editor Casey Kittrell at the University of Texas Press, whose sense of humor and good instincts have made *Woman Walk the Line* even better. And if we're only as good as our editor, Lynne Chapman opted not to farm this collection out, but to edit it herself.

Obviously, I owe a massive debt to the women who contributed. In the midst of their own towering obligations, health challenges, family needs, and other writing projects, they made time to consider these artists, their own lives, and what it all means. "Thank you" doesn't begin to cover it.

Dan Einstein, Wendy Pearl, Missy Staggs, and the non-reading Kathie Orrico were all sounding boards and friends who listened, fed me, laughed, and kept me focused throughout this process. Andrea Billups and Michael McCall evaluated and embraced the notion. Charles L. Pickett Jr. was the extra eyes and the comma checker for a dyslexic editrix trying to keep up with a flurry of writers. Burt Stein provided counsel and calm in the storm. The Rock & Roll Hall of Fame and the Country Music Hall of Fame deserve major thank yous for the use of their libraries. Also, thanks to Pinewood Social, Fido, Laurel School, Prestis Bakery, Barney's Beanery in West Hollywood, Delray Dunes Golf Club, Surfside, Testas, the late Michael McCartys, and Greens Pharmacy for providing places to assign, edit, write, and ponder during the many months of gestation. Finally, appreciation to Buddy Miller for the advice, and Kenny Chesney—of all people—for having the faith that I could do this in the middle of tours, album setups, and a whole lot of music. As he said, "Wow, that's so smart!"

Nonlinear shout-outs go to the Spaulding University MFA Program, and especially Kathy Mann, for loving country music; Kathleen Driskell for believing you can make anything work; Katy Yocom for the spark; Rebecca Walker and Rachel Harper for showing the way; and Dianne Aprile for sensitivity, depth, and always going to the heart. Also, thanks to Ann Powers and Evelyn McDonnell, whose *Rock She Wrote* pioneered the power of collected women's voices celebrating music and musical artists so many years ago, and Tom DeSavia and John Doe for their inspiring *Under the Big Black Sun*, another very tangible reminder of the potency of many voices celebrating the same thing. Finally, Doug Adrianson, my long-ago editor at the *Miami Herald*, deserves a special thank you for always asking, "Yes, but what more do you need to say?"

And to Rosanne Cash and Emmylou Harris, two of the brightest lights on my own musical journey: your willingness to make lyrics matter, and to bare messy emotions over music that often blurred not just expectations but genre lines, enraptured me; thank you for the gift of thinking beyond what I knew. I was never meant to like—or respond to—country music, but somehow you were my gateway drugs.

So many women writers weren't available or able to contribute to this volume. So many subjects, including Tammy

Wynnette, Reba McEntire, the Dixie Chicks, Miranda Lambert, Patsy Cline, Faith Hill, Deborah Allen, Marshall Chapman, Jessie Colter, and Lee Ann Womack, remain. Perhaps these are the seeds for another volume. Or maybe you will be moved to write your own homage to that artist who touched and transformed you. Music, like water, often moves and shapes us without our ever realizing it; let this be an opening for your own consideration.

CONTRIBUTORS

Author of *The Food Activist Handbook: Big & Small Things You Can Do to Help Provide Fresh, Healthy Food for Your Community*, Wisconsin-born **ALI BERLOW** is a mother, wife, friend, author, and independent radio producer living these days in the northeast. As the founder of the Island Grown Initiative, Berlow connected farmers and consumers, as well as launching Island Grown Schools to reinforce school lunch programs with sustainable elements.

One of the country's preeminent singer-songwriters, **ROSANNE CASH** has released fifteen albums of songs that have earned four Grammy awards and nominations for eleven more, as well as twenty-one Top 40 hits, including eleven No. 1 singles. She is also an author, whose four books include the best-selling memoir *Composed*. Her essays have appeared in, among other places, the *New York Times*, *Rolling Stone*, the *Oxford American*, and the *Nation*. In addition to touring continually, Cash has partnered in programming collaborations with Carnegie Hall, Lincoln Center, San Francisco Jazz, the Minnesota Orchestra, and the Library of Congress. She served as 2015 Artist-in-Residence at the Country Music Hall of Fame and Museum in Nashville, and in 2015 she was inducted into the Nashville Songwriters Hall of Fame.

KANDIA CRAZY HORSE is a country & western singer-songwriter who has explored her southern roots on the albums *Stampede* and *Canyons*. Previously, she served as a rock critic and music editor for outlets including the *Village Voice*, the *San Francisco Bay Guardian*, and *Creative Loafing*, with a focus on the second wave of southern rock and Americana. Based in Manhattan, she leads the Native Americana band Cactus Rose.

A former music and theater critic at *USA Today*, **ELYSA GARDNER** was also—at different, often overlapping, points—a regular contributor to the *Los Angeles Times*, *Rolling Stone*, and the *New Yorker*'s "Night Life" section. She has written for the *New York Times*, *Harper's*, *Out*, *Town & Country*, *Entertainment Weekly*, *Spin*, and *Vibe*, and served on the jury for the 2015 Pulitzer Prize in drama. She lives in New York City.

A two-time Grammy nominee and an award-winning writer, editor, and music consultant, **HOLLY GEORGE-WARREN** was named one of the top women music critics "you need to read" by Flavorwire.com. She is the author of sixteen books, including *A Man Called Destruction: The Life and Music of Alex Chilton, from the Box Tops to Big Star to Backdoor Man*; *Public Cowboy No. 1: The Life and Times of Gene Autry*; and a forthcoming biography of Janis Joplin. Other recent books include the *New York Times* best seller *The Road to Woodstock* (with Michael Lang) and *John Varvatos: Rock in Fashion* (with Varvatos).

HOLLY GLEASON is a music critic, academic, and artist development consultant. She has written extensively for *Rolling Stone*, the *Los Angeles Times*, the *Miami Herald*, *Paste*, *Musician*, the *Oxford American*, *No Depression*, *Lone Star Music*, and *Hits*. A 2016 Rock & Roll Hall of Fame/Case Western Reserve for the Study of Pop Music fellowship recipient and a nominee for Best Cultural Reporting by the International Network of Street Papers, she is currently working on *Even Cowgirls Get the Blues*, an Emmylou Harris biography, for the University of Texas Press's American Music Series.

A winner of the Nashville Songwriters Hall of Fame "I Wish I Wrote That Song" Award, **LADY GOODMAN** has frequented the fringes and shadows of roots music since her childhood. "Just To Watch Maria Dance," which she co-wrote with the legendary Guy Clark, is one of three unreleased songs on *Guy Clark: The Best of the DualTone Years*.

NANCY HARRISON has spent more than twenty-five years as an entertainment news journalist, working at *E!* and *Extra* and freelancing for the *New York Times*. In 1996, she helped launch *Access Hollywood*, where she has overseen the show's music coverage since 2005. In her more than two decades in the business, she has interviewed some of the most influential artists in pop, rock, hip-hop, and country.

RONNI LUNDY is the author of *Victuals: An Appalachian Journey, with Recipes* (Clarkson Potter, 2016), which won the 2017 James Beard Award for Cookbook of the Year. She has been writing about the food, music, and culture of the southern Appalachians and the American South for more than thirty years. A founding member of the Southern Foodways Alliance, she has been an editor and/or writer for newspapers (*Louisville Times/Courier Journal*) and magazines (*Esquire, Gourmet, Eating Well*), and an editor at Lark Books. She has written or edited numerous other books, including *Shuck Beans, Stack Cakes, and Honest Fried Chicken* (Atlantic, 1990), named by *Gourmet* as one of the six essential cookbooks on Southern food.

A journalist and feminist music critic based in Dallas, Texas, **AMY ELIZABETH McCARTHY** has published her writing in *Playboy, Pitchfork, Texas Monthly*, the *Houston Press*, and Salon.

In her nearly thirty years in the music business, **KELLY McCARTNEY** has worked in a myriad of capacities with a multitude of artists. Since 2014, she has focused on music journalism, serving as the managing editor for the Bluegrass Situation and freelancing for Folk Alley, NPR Music, *Curve*, and *No Depression*.

Over the twenty years that **SHELBY MORRISON** has worked in the music industry, her focus has been on museums, including the Buddy Holly Center, where she worked closely with Holly's estate; the B. B. King Museum, where she served as a research assistant; and the Rock & Roll Hall of Fame, where she has produced exhibits and fostered artist relationships for the last dozen years. She has also worked as a music research consultant for Becker & Mayer Publishing and a contributing writer for exhibits at Midwestern State University. Currently, she is the Director of Artist & VIP Relations at the Rock & Roll Hall of Fame.

MEREDITH OCHS is an award-winning radio talk show host, commentator, DJ, author, musician, and photographer. She is heard regularly on Sirius XM and National Public Radio, and her work has appeared in numerous places, including *Entertainment Weekly*, *Rolling Stone*, and Salon.

Garden & Gun's Asssistant Online Editor, **DACEY ORR**, had a varied career working in multimedia production, promotions, touring, and events before settling on journalism in 2012. A former editor at *Paste*, she has contributed to such publications and websites as the *Village Voice*, the Bluegrass Situation, *Vice*, and Stereogum.

Currently the Country Music Association's vice president of corporate communications, **WENDY PEARL** has had a career that included stints as a radio music director and a reporter for CNN's startup Miami bureau. She spent nearly a decade with the *Miami Herald*, where she participated in the paper's Pulitzer Prize–winning coverage of the first Gulf War (1991). Arriving in Nashville in 1992, Pearl handled publicity and artist development at Sony Music and Asylum Records before joining the Country Music Association in 2000.

Grammy-nominated **GRACE POTTER** has straddled roots, hard rock, blues, country, and pop music since founding Grace Potter and the Nocturnals at St. Lawrence University. With six records to her credit, including 2015's solo *Midnight*, the Vermont-born force of nature, known for high-energy shows featuring her own B-3 organ and Flying V electric guitar playing, has become a festival favorite, and has shared stages with the Rolling Stones and Gov't Mule.

ALICE RANDALL is a foremother of transgressive feminist country. In songs ranging from the simple "Small Towns (Are Smaller for Girls)" and "God's a Woman" to more complex narratives, such as "The Ballad of Sally Anne"—in which a black bride holds a white community responsible for the lynching of her groom—she has told necessary untold stories. As a novelist, she has taken on equally challenging territory: her first novel, *The Wind Done Gone*, reimagined black and white lives on the plantation Tara. With over thirty recorded songs and four published novels, the Harvard graduate and *New York Times* best-selling author is also the only black woman to write a No. 1 country song, "XXX's and OOO's (An American Girl)." She is currently a professor and writer-in-residence at Vanderbilt University.

CARYN ROSE is a New York City–based writer and photographer who documents rock & roll and urban life. She is the author of two novels (*B-Sides and Broken Hearts* and *A Whole New Ballgame*) and three nonfiction books (including *Raise Your Hand*, a document of Bruce Springsteen's 2012 European tour). She is also a contributor to Pitchfork, MTV News, Salon, *Billboard*, the

Village Voice, Vulture, the Guardian, NPR, *Backstreets Magazine,* and *Brooklyn Magazine,* among others.

KIM RUEHL spent her twenties chasing the singer-songwriter dream before she fell into a career writing about other people's music. Since 2005, her work has appeared in print and online at *Billboard, Yes,* NPR, the Bluegrass Situation, and elsewhere. In 2008 she became news editor of *No Depression,* the roots music journal, and has been instrumental in ushering that publication through many evolutions. Currently she is *ND*'s editor-in-chief. She lives in Asheville, North Carolina.

The executive editor at *People Magazine,* **CYNTHIA SANZ** is a lifelong fan of country music. In more than two decades at the magazine, she has chronicled the careers of Nashville legends and newcomers, as well as overseeing coverage of such topics as television and crime. In 2006, she founded the brand's *People Country* franchise, and she is the 2009 recipient of the Country Music Association's Media Recognition Award. A native of San Antonio, Texas, Sanz graduated summa cum laude from the University of Texas at Austin and previously worked at the *New York Times* and the *Dallas Morning News.* She lives on Long Island.

The catalyst for "garage country," **AUBRIE SELLERS** released her debut *New City Blues* to critical acclaim from *Rolling Stone, Garden & Gun,* the *New York Times,* and NPR. The next-wave songwriter and guitarist has also sung on albums by Dr. Ralph Stanley, David Nail, and Miranda Lambert. She currently lives in East Nashville.

The author of *Record Collecting for Girls,* **COURTNEY E. SMITH** is an editor at Refinery29. She started in the music business as an intern at MTV, eventually working her way into the music programming department, where she focused on indie rock. She has worked at CBS and iHeartRadio and has been published by Pitchfork, Lenny Letter, and *Billboard.*

DEBORAH SPRAGUE has gone through a lot of changes since getting her first paid byline, while still in junior high, in inner-city Cleveland. Over the course of the last three decades she has served as editor at *CREEM*; a critic for the *New York Daily News, Newsday,* and *Variety*; and a contributor to *Rolling Stone, Spin, Billboard,* and more than a dozen other publications. Her work has also appeared in collections, such as *Kill Your Idols: A New Generation of Rock Writers Reconsiders the Classics* (Barricade Books). She lives in Queens, New York.

The singer, songwriter, musician, and producer **TAYLOR SWIFT** is a ten-time Grammy winner; the youngest recipient in history of the music industry's highest honor, the Grammy for Album of the Year; and the only female in the history of the Grammys to win Album of the Year twice. She is the only artist in history to have an album hit the million-copy mark in first-week sales three times (with 2010's *Speak Now*, 2012's *Red*, and 2014's *1989*). She was twice *Billboard*'s Woman of the Year, one of *Time*'s 100 Most Influential People in the World, and one of only eight candidates for *Time*'s Person of the Year in 2014.

MADISON VAIN is a music correspondent for *Entertainment Weekly*. After attending Wake Forest University, she moved to New York City to pursue journalism and quickly found a home at *Sports Illustrated*. From there, she moved down the hall to *EW*.

A cookbook author, young adult novelist, and poet, **CAROLINE RANDALL WILLIAMS** received her MFA from the University of Mississippi, where she coauthored the Phillis Wheatley Award–winning *The Diary of B. B. Bright, Possible Princess* and the NAACP Image Award–winning *Soul Food Love*. A Cave Canem fellow, she has had poetry featured in several journals, including the *Iowa Review*, the *Massachusetts Review*, and *Palimpsest*. Her debut poetry collection, *Lucy Negro, Redux*, was published by Ampersand Books in 2015. She is currently writer-in-residence at Fisk University.

A reporter for the *Washington Post*, **EMILY YAHR** covers pop culture and entertainment for the Style section. She joined the *Post* in 2008, shortly after she graduated from the University of Maryland with a degree in journalism. A native of Cleveland, she currently lives in Washington, DC.